ADVANCED

FILM & VIDEO

PRODUCTION

College Production series

Advanced Film and Video Production

Advanced Film and Video Production

Introduction

Film or video production for students is an opportunity to express creativity in exciting ways. Like any new language, there are basic principals that should be taught and understood before that expression can be fully realized. Students starting a broadcast production class are excited about the hands-on experience. For that reason, there will be a desire to get started right away. The difficulty will be to hold back long enough to learn the basic tools needed in order to communicate with others on productions.

Film and video production is a group effort with each student performing a vital task for the good of the overall objective. It is imperative that cooperation among students be taught as one of the necessary skills involved in productions. In some cases, this will be as simple as help with lighting or camerawork and at other times as complex as help with scenery design or special effects make-up.

The text of this production book has been compiled from over thirty years of hands-on work in the professional film and television industry with some of the most successful production specialists in "Hollywood", followed by teaching production techniques at Columbia College in Los Angeles, California.

Careful attention has been paid to how to teach students at various levels of initial understanding. For some, the beginning will seem almost too basic, for others it will seem too complex. In order to reach a happy medium, the text has been designed to give rudimentary concepts in all phases of production at the beginning and then return to those same concepts later in the book in more detail and with more complexity. Although the material has been created for college level classes, high schools can use this text if used along with a teacher's supplemental teaching guide without learning complications for the student. The material covered is not difficult to understand for any young person who has grown up watching movies and television. The entire text for high schools may be spread over one year with more time spent on each chapter. For college level classes this material may be covered in two semesters or less depending on the time spent in lab situation assignments.

This book has been designed to prepare students for the real world of television and film work in an industry that demands professional skills and attitudes. For that reason, the learning path created in this text is the same path used by any professional production embarking on a commercial venture. By using the procedures used by professionals, students learn worthy habits from the beginning, so that whether they use these skills for a career in the production business or to create professional looking video presentations for their future corporate in-house needs, they are prepared for prospective broadcast productions.

Because the author over the span of his career was both a filmmaker and a video production producer and director, the terms "filmmaker" and "filmmaking" are used interchangeably with "video production" throughout the book. The reason for this is we have seen so much change in the last decade in the art of filmmaking through the use of video, computer animation and computer special effects. Filmmaking is an art form that we all enjoy and to reserve the term to only apply when film stock is used would not fully express the art form as it relates to what it entails today and in the near future.

It is the intent of this book on production to fully prepare you to make your own feature film when this course is completed, should you so choose.

Chapter One

Film and Video Production as *Filmmaking*

Within the framework of video production that is often thought of as simply filmmaking, we can readily see that there are two distinct halves, in front of the camera and behind the camera. We will examine both sides for an understanding of what both entail.

For those who are interested in some phase of production work behind the camera, there are three basic divisions; pre-production, production and postproduction. And within those segments there are still finer divisions that include everything from script writing and location scouting to final movie posters and advertising. One can become quite successful in any one of the many phases of film production without having the need to do it all.

Let us begin by listing some of the job classifications you have seen on film credits and group them into the various departments.

- ☐ Executive producer, producer, line producer, associate producer.
- ☐ Director, first assistant director, second assistant director.
- ☐ Second unit director, stunt coordinator, stunt players.
- ☐ Director of photography, camera operator, assistant camera, gaffer, best boy, electrician.
- ☐ Key grip, grips.
- ☐ Production designer, art director, assistant art director, draftsperson, construction coordinator, head carpenter, set decorator, property master, prop person, wardrobe, make up, hair.

- ☐ Model makers, miniatures
- ☐ Special effects coordinator, special effects person.
- ☐ Actors, dialogue coach, script supervisor, background players (extras).
- ☐ Animal handlers.
- ☐ Vehicles and on-camera transportation devices.
- ☐ Sound recorder, boom operator, sound mixer.

This is just a brief list of the many job categories that make up a production team on a professional film. In addition to these who's work will be seen on camera there are countless others who's work is not directly seen but are a vital part of the group. Transportation drivers, catering, crafts service people, gophers(go for this, deliver that), accountants, secretaries, writers, editors, music composers, sound effects designers, computer animators, and production assistants and interns for all of the various departments play a crucial part in bringing a finished film to a theatre near you.

Actors in the filmmaking class

Some students have an interest in acting and perhaps feel that a discussion on the aspects of filmmaking is not important. Let's consider this possibility by directly speaking to actors in the group.

When you are acting in a school play you have learned your lines, rehearsed, and you have been directed and coached in the best way to create the character you want to portray. When you step out on the stage you are at the same time alone and free to do as you please. The strokes that you paint on your canvass for the audience are much broader and more forgiving. Your timeline is linear and connected. Filmmaking is none of those things. Without a good understanding of all the aspects of the filmmaking process as a young actor working on a real movie, you will be at the mercy of total strangers who may not have your best interest at heart. They do have <u>their</u> best interest at heart, and you may find your performance on the cutting room floor for no better reason than you had no idea what was going on around you. It is so difficult to win an Oscar when your best performance ended up edited out of the final film. Actors have been cut out of scenes for a number of reasons. So it is important to understand why you want to learn as much as possible so that you may avoid some of those reasons.

The Most Important Job

The art of filmmaking is one of collaboration with all the others who are working with you. Who has the most important job on a movie set? <u>Everyone</u> has the most important job for the simple reason that if you take that person's job away you have an incomplete picture. Any one of those jobs that can bring a production to a standstill is the most important job at that moment. It is critical to see that filmmaking is a team effort with all departments working together.

In the Beginning was the Word

The place to begin any film or video project is the written word in the form of a script. A  script can be as simple as an outline of where you want to go with your story, or as complex as detailed instructions on how the set should look and how the actor should react. Even the thirty-second commercial has a story to tell. You should not break the rules unless you know the rules, so it is important to learn the rules of storytelling. Now, we are about to embark on a wonderful adventure of storytelling. The first step in this adventure is to brainstorm ideas and place those concepts in a logical order on paper so that we can see before the camera rolls the first time if we have met our goals.

Every story has a beginning, middle and an end. That is an easy way to look at the very complex process of scriptwriting. Television network executives who have the power to put your project on the air will tell you that every good story should be able to be explained in one sentence or two. This is called a story's premise. Pick up a *TV Guide* and read some random storyline premises listed under the show's title.

The Secret Formula

There is a formula for telling your story. No matter how unique you feel your story is, it can be condensed down to one sentence that fits a formula. What happens if you go against the formula? Your  audience loses interest early on or hates the way your story ends. For example, the formula for romantic stories would be as follows:

- ☐ Boy *meets* girl. (Premise)
- ☐ Boy *gets* girl. (Act one)
- ☐ Boy *loses* girl (Act two)
- ☐ Boy *gets girl **back*** again. (Act three)

Think about some movies you have seen that were romantic stories and you will notice that it is true. The only real variation being after he gets her back again, one of them dies for the good of their cause. Audiences seldom like this variation, however. Obviously the formula can be reversed to *girl gets boy*, but you get the idea, it is still the same formula. In a later chapter on screenwriting we will discuss in detail the formula for dramatic stories. You may be surprised to find out the simple formula that has worked in Hollywood for decades.

In dramatic storytelling you have two basic character types, the protagonist and the antagonist. In its simplest form, the protagonist is the hero and the antagonist is the villain. You certainly can have a story with more than one protagonist and even more than one antagonist. You can even have more than one storyline. In Hollywood, for episodic TV programs, it even has a name. It is called the 'A' story and the 'B' story. *CSI (Crime Scene Investigators)* on CBS is a good example of this type of storytelling. *ER and Family Law* are others. If you think about it, most of the programs you have grown up watching have been done this way. As we explain the basic steps for creating a script, you should apply these concepts to your project. The little extra time spent on the subject now will save much more time later with the efficient use of your time for your project.

The beginning. If you analyze most of the popular action-adventure, drama and horror movies over the last few decades you will see that they have one thing in common. The story almost never begins with what is called in the industry as 'back story'. How does it begin? It begins in the middle of an action scene. *Raiders of the Lost Ark* begins how? Does it begin with a scene where we find out Indiana Jones is an Archeologist at a university? No, it begins with some guy we don't know in a fedora and kaki pants about to get into serious trouble, followed by more trouble, and just when we think he is in the clear, even more trouble. This is called a *scene sequence*. This scene sequence continues until we are on the edge of our seats and the sequence is played out. *Then* we find out Indiana Jones is a professor in a university. Why? Because the storyteller wants to grab our attention before he gives us the important but somewhat dull back-story. The storyteller is saying: "Look, you're in for a great ride, so fasten your safety belt and watch out." Most Hollywood professionals believe that you need to grab the attention of your audience within the first five-percent of your program length. In a thirty-second spot, that's two seconds. In a ten-minute video, that's thirty-seconds. In a two-hour movie that's the first six minutes. Six minutes is a very long time on film. What is the next thing you need to tell your audience in the beginning? In a very simplistic way, the beginning of a story should serve what important purposes?

☐   We establish the kind of story we are about to tell.

☐   We establish the characters we want our audience to know.

☐   We present the audience with our premise.

☐   We create a reason for our audience to keep watching or become more interested.

For the type of programs you are about to create, the beginning should serve the purpose of presenting your problem to the audience. And again, it should be one clear direct sentence. There are a number of items which are more complex and serve the purpose of telling a good dramatic story which are beyond the scope of this text for now and will be explained in chapter twenty two.

The middle of our script should ask the audience some questions and present ways of solving the problem we have presented in the beginning. The middle is the main body of the program. If you allow yourself to indulge too long with the presenting of the problem, you run the risk of losing your audience altogether. In their mind they begin to say: "This is too overwhelming." and tune out. It is important to see the progress of the story and know when you have spent too much time on the problem without offering any help, or shown too many examples of the problem without offering any possible solutions. The audience begins to say to themselves: "Okay, I get your point, let's move on, for Pete's sake!"

The middle of our story fulfills these important needs:

☐ We intensify the problem through examples.
☐ We allow our audience to ask questions mentally from the material we have presented.

The end of your story is the wrap up. You have presented your problem, you have shown examples of the problem and now you need to present solutions, hope and some kind of resolve for good or bad in the case of a dramatic story. For commercials and public service announcements (PSA), we have what is called in the advertising business, as *the call to action*. You have been subjected to the 'call to action' most of your lives while watching commercials. The typical: "If you call in the next fifteen minutes, we will send you *two* of these really crumby things that won't actually work." Or:

"Don't miss out on this great offer, come by today..." (Because we may be out of business tomorrow if you don't!)

Very often commercials have at the end what is commonly called the "tag". Sometimes this is a comic punch line to the story set up in the spot. Recapping what we have just covered, consider the following aspects of the writing process:

☐ What is the purpose of the script?

☐ What are the various elements of the script?

☐ What is the importance of the wrap up?

☐ What is the call to action?

We have now completed an important step in the creation of a video production; we have simplified the complex art of screenwriting into something that you can do by yourself. Next, we will break down the difficult task of preparing and shooting a video production into several very basic steps that you can do in a very professional way, once you know the secrets.

The Importance of an Outline

One of the best ways to start a script is to begin with an outline. The outline should be a simple road map of where you want to go in your presentation. To start that process ask yourself the following questions:

☐ What is the purpose of the production?

☐ What are the basic elements of the production?

☐ Does the story lead to a climax, and some resolve? [In the case of a dramatic story]

☐ Does the production lead to a call to action? [In the case of a spot or PSA]

Once these basic elements are solidified in your mind the story will begin to take shape. With practice, this process will become much more easy in time.

Example assignment: Create a thirty second PSA (Public Service Announcement) on the importance of not doing drugs. [Other choices can be substituted]

☐ What is the purpose of the production?

To reduce the problems created by drugs at your school.

☐ What are the basic elements of the production?

Why should anyone care if you do drugs? Present the problem. Show examples of the problem.

☐ Does the production lead to a call to action? Offer solutions. Present the call to action.

Humor is a great way of getting a point across to your audience and this is an ideal production in which to use humor. Think of some funny situations that can be shown without the need for dialogue or voice over. Some 'dude' wiped out in class, falling down in front of the instructor, asleep in their locker. Humor is *reality* taken to the *extreme*. In this case, it could be presented as a national epidemic, with the need to call out the National Guard, or state police. Teens being hauled off to jail, their lives ruined because of it. Brainstorm your own ways of showing this to your audience, using the resources you have at hand including the use of animals, or anything that will present this idea to your audience if you do not have actors and special props. Be inventive and remember that there are no wrong answers, just some that show more ingenuity and creativity.

More example assignments

Make a music video using:

Natural wildlife as subject a matter.

A trip to a local Zoo or animals you find in your

neighborhood.

Using other students at school or people at a shopping mall or businesses.

First Projects

Music videos are an especially easy way to begin learning both the art of shooting video and editing your raw footage. Many students want to get started right away with editing the

footage they have shot and believe they can just put down their video footage first and then "cut" their audio (in this case, music) second. Nothing could be more wrong in approaching editing. For this entry level of editing you will not be editing music, so it will be put down in one pass as a single edit. Your visuals must be edited to your music and therefore the music is laid down first, then followed with your various video edits. In a later chapter we will cover editing in more detail.

The Importance of a Script

Once you have created an outline and have some solid ideas about what you want to shoot, it is time to convert your ideas to a script. Without a script your actors and crew have no idea what you want to accomplish in your  production. The page layout for a typical video production script need not be complicated. It can be as simple as dialogue and voice over information on the left side of the page and a description of the video on the right side of the page. It helps to have some form of a drawing of the video in a frame indicating the frame of the camera. [See illustrations] If you are not an artist, even simple stick figures will get the point across to your cast and crew.

A simple stick figure storyboard

Sample Audio/Video Script Page:

Your Production Company		**Client:**	
Audio Scene #		**Video** Scene #	
1	EXT. Sidewalk - Day **JILL** (Singing Lyrics) Oh, Jack, I only want to be with you. **JACK** (Singing Lyrics) Oh, Jill, you say that now, but what about tomorrow? Dissolve to Close Up	1	Jill walks up to Jack
2		2	

In learning the language of film and video it is important to be able to communicate in common terms that your cast and crew will understand both on the printed script page and verbally on the 'set'. With the exposure that most young people have from watching movies and television many of the following terms will be familiar to you, some you might not be sure about and others perhaps you have never heard.

Camera Terms

Wide shot-This shot shows the audience as much of the total picture of the scene as you want them to see. Typically, this is an establishing shot so that the audience knows

where the story takes place. A shot of the whole city from a distance or a shot that shows the whole room.

Medium shot-This shot is a closer version of the wide shot and brings us closer to our subject or subject matter. In the case of an actor, it is usually a shot that includes the head and

shoulders of the actor. In the case of subject matter, it could be a shot of just a book, sitting on a desk.

Close up shot- Is just that, close up. Usually Containing only the face of the actor. In the case of subject matter, it might be a close up view of one line written on a page of the book.

Insert shot-This term is used both in shooting and editing. It is a close up shot of something important to the storyline. The actor types something on a keypad, which we are able to see closely for some story point reason.

Reverse angle-shows what is going on behind the camera's present angle. An example might

be two views of a country road. Where the trees and shade are on the left of frame shading toward the right of frame in the first angle and in the reverse angle the trees

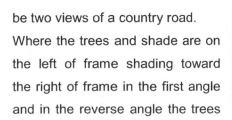

are on the right of frame shading toward the left frame.

Establishing shot - Although listed above, it is an important term to understand. The establishing shot conveys information to your audience that a wide shot might not convey. Each new location should have an establishing shot so that your audience knows where you are at this point in the story.

Pan-Turning the camera right or left while mounted on a tripod or handheld.

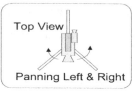

Tilt-Pointing the camera up or down while mounted on a tripod or handheld.

Dolly shot-Moving the camera on a dolly or wheeled tripod in closer or out further from the subject.

Trucking shot-Moving the dolly or wheeled tripod sideways from the subject.

Zoom-Using the camera's zoom lens ability to bring the subject closer or farther away without moving the tripod.

Rack focus-Changing the focus from one distance to another. Often used to emphasize the importance of one character over another. The arrow in the illustration indicates the change

Rack Focus

of focus from the actor in the background to the actor in the foreground.

Aspect ratio-The relationship of the height of the frame with the width. The normal aspect ratio of standard television is 3:4 (3 units high by 4 units wide) The HDTV aspect ratio is 9:16 (9 units high by 16 units wide).

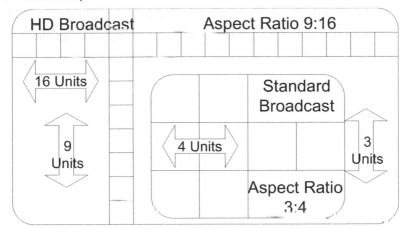

Dolly-A platform with wheels on which the camera is mounted for moving the camera during a shot.

Angle-A script term to indicate a basic description of where the camera is pointing.

INT.- A script term short for "Interior". This tells your reader the action takes place inside a building.

EXT.- A script term short for "exterior". This tells your reader the action takes place outside a building or simply outdoors.

Class Assignment

Record several TV commercials from off the air in your locale, then critique them in class as a group.

What works in the commercials?

What does not work in the commercials?

What was the premise?

What was the call to action?

What was the tag for the commercial?

Once the professional spots have been critiqued, the student projects should be analyzed in the same way, searching for originality, clarity, and professionalism.

Chapter Two

Getting Started

Once your script has been completed you are ready for the next phase of your production that is called pre-production. In the motion picture and television industry this phase is most important to reduce unnecessary expenses due to ill prepared  pre-production. As you examine your shooting script you will discover all the needs of your story, such as: actors, locations, props, set pieces or vehicles, lighting needs, and crew requirements.

Your first production will probably be very simple in concept and execution and may be nothing more than you and the camera and "shopping list" of shots to get for editing later, so your pre-production may be only to accurately list the shots that you will need. As your productions become more involved, more attention will be required to insure that your shoots are organized. Nothing is worse than showing up at a location with all of your actors and crew ready to begin and realize no one thought to bring video tape for the camera or the necessary cords for recording sound, or some special prop the actor is to hold or handle. Check lists are vitally important for avoiding these kinds of problems. If you are shooting in the broadcast department of your school where all of the equipment is stored, it is no problem to get that extra piece of equipment you forgot, but if you have checked the equipment out for a weekend shoot at someone's home or business, you've just wasted your whole weekend and your cast and crew's time as well. There is no excuse for poor pre-production. Good pre-production is the outgrowth of studying your script to determine that every aspect has been considered in advance. Should you continue your interest in production as a career, these professional habits you acquire now will put you ahead in working on professional shoots in the motion picture and television industry. It is sometimes difficult for students to understand why Algebra is important in life or History or even English Literature, and it may be years before you finally appreciate them, so the scope of this text is to prepare you for the real and practical world of production work right out of school, giving you skills you will need immediately. For that reason it is important that we cover these many basic and sometimes complicated elements and aspects of preparing a simple shoot.

Pre-production Considerations
- ☐ Script requirements for cast and crew.
- ☐ Camera, lighting and sound requirements.
- ☐ Art department requirements such as props, set pieces, wardrobe, make-up, hair, location and special effects.
- ☐ Transportation and food, if required.
- ☐ Animal handling.
- ☐ Shooting schedule and coordination.

For your first productions the thought of doing detailed pre-production seems unnecessary, but it is the habit of doing careful pre-production preparation that is important. Later on you will be glad you took the time to analyze your script in pre-production and learned how, when your productions become more involved and complicated.

Production Considerations

Once your pre-production phase has been completed it is time to begin your production phase. Before that starts, it is wise to take one more look at your script. Have you discovered during pre-production that something called for in the script is not possible or available? Now is the time to change the script, not during the shoot, when everyone is standing around waiting for directions.

Surprisingly, students not familiar with production techniques assume that scenes are shot chronologically, that is, the way a scene plays out if it were a stage play. Because of lighting considerations and camera locations changes, it is not practical to move the camera for one actor's close up and then back to the other actor's close up and so on and so on. It is much more efficient to shoot all of the camera angles in one direction and move the camera to the next angle and shoot all on those angles. In editing, these pieces are put in their proper chronological order.

In preparing the equipment for a shoot the camera department should set the camera, tripod, batteries, monitors and mics up for a test record to see that everything is in good working order. Once it has been determined to be in working condition, then break down the equipment and pack it for the location shoot. Following this procedure will greatly reduce your chances of forgotten cords, batteries or recording media at the time of the shoot.

What to Shoot First

One of the first considerations you should be concerned with as you begin your shoot is what to shoot first. If it is a dramatic recreation of two actors talking, you know you will want a wide shot and two close ups, so that you can later edit the actors best work into one tight scene. Often, in shooting such a scene which may be out doors or have the sun coming in a window, you may need to shoot the wide shot first (Just in case you lose the sun later). Two good reasons for this are: You can fake the sun in close ups with lights (If you have to) and you establish the action in the wide shot which is easier to match with the close ups. Your actors remember what they did in the wide shot and can easily duplicate it in the closer shots, as well as the fact that you can see how the scene works overall in the wide shot. If you shot the close ups first and later discovered in the wide shot that something did not work, you then would have a matching problem and need to re-shoot the close ups again. Your actors are going to be doing the scene at least three times as it is, so the more you can avoid making them do it again, the better.

Post Production Considerations

Although editing will be handled in a later chapter in detail, there are some basic concepts that should be addressed at this point in order to avoid problems later when you begin to edit your first production. As part of this wonderfully creative language that you are beginning to discover, there are aspects of filmmaking that you may never have been aware before taking this course when you watched TV programs or movies. As you become more aware of these concepts and watch professional productions, these concepts will seem to jump off the screen at you. And yet, they were there all along for you to discover, if only you had known about them.

Following the Rules

In editing any presentation you create, there are certain rules that should be followed. Some are so subtle that almost no one would notice if wrong, others are so obvious that your presentation is ruined if you make such a mistake.

These rules have a long history in the art of editing that is part of the language of film. They were established before "talkies" came into existence and they have outlasted many generations of film and videotape editors. With each generation of young editors there is a tendency to do it in a completely new way. They hope to reinvent editing by breaking all the old rules because they have not taken the time to learn these tried and true rules. All these beginners are doing is reinventing the wheel. Their time would be much better spent learning the rules and becoming proficient editors first. First and foremost, an editor should be invisible.

The 180° Rule

If you imagine an invisible line running perpendicular to the camera's view, you can readily see that this line runs between your two actors. [See illustration next page] This line is called your action line or 180° line. This expression comes from the 360° circle that makes up the space in front of you in plan.

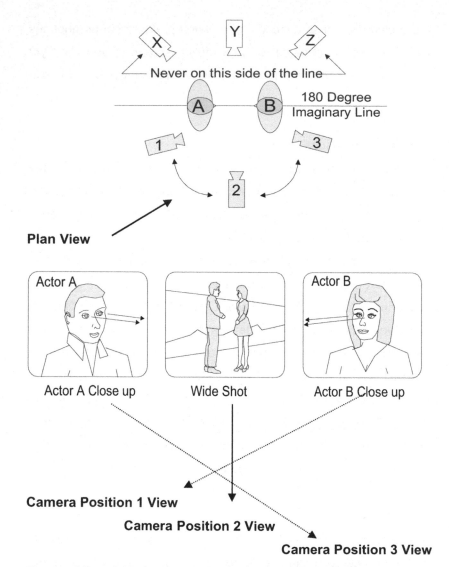

Plan View

Actor A Close up   Wide Shot   Actor B Close up

Camera Position 1 View

Camera Position 2 View

Camera Position 3 View

Proper Use of 180° Rule - Staying on One Side of Imaginary
Line

The camera is placed anywhere on the side between the actors and the camera's position, and the actors can be anywhere on the other side of that line (Or on that line). If the camera ever crosses that line the actor will appear on screen as looking in the wrong direction at the other actor. [See illustration below] This is called the one eighty rule. You must always be aware of this imaginary line and careful not to cross it. There are ways of breaking this rule by establishing a new action line, but for now just learn the rule and do not create editing problems for yourself by crossing the line.

Improper Use of 180° Rule

Not Staying on One Side of Imaginary Line

The 180° Rule Continued:

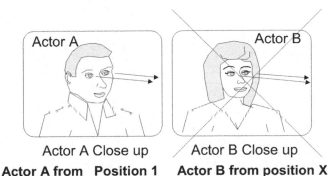

Actor A Close up   Actor B Close up

Actor A from   Position 1   Actor B from position X

By crossing the imaginary line for camera position **X**

Subject no longer appears to be looking at Actor A.

Dimensional Thinking

When you photograph anything in the real world and put it on video or a photograph, maybe without realizing it, you are converting it from three dimensions to two. Your picture is flat. If you put your actors flat against a wall and

photograph them, you compound the flatness, so it is important to make your picture composition more dynamic by creating more depth to your backgrounds. This will be covered in detail later, but for now, remember that you want the scenery around your actors or subject matter to look as three dimensional as possible by placing the camera so that it sees the wall at an angle in relationship to the camera.

Four examples of various angles that can increase the perspective or flatten out the perspective of the frame.

The Sydney Opera House, Sydney, Australia

Getting the Coverage

One of the reasons for shooting so many different angles in a motion picture is not because the director is not sure which is best, it is to give the editor choices in the editing phase. Sometimes a portion of the scene is best expressed with a wide shot so that the audience is able to see other action the actor is reacting to at the moment. Other portions of the scene may be best expressed with a close up of the actor's face. So it is important to cover the action from different angles and a variety of shots such as close ups, medium shots and wide shots so that you have some choices when you begin the editing phase. Since your first productions will be more simplistic in nature it is easy to forget these rules, but remember to get this same kind of coverage with those assignments as well. For example, if your first production is a music video in which you are editing footage of many ducks in a pond as a key element of your theme, then it would be good to get wide shots of several ducks floating together, single shots of one duck, a close up of the duck's head, and so on. Later in editing, you will have a lot of raw footage from which to choose key shots that tell your story.

It is important to keep in mind that you are seeing things as you shoot, that you may not be showing your audience what is vital for them to know about in order to be able to follow the story you are trying to tell. Sometimes this visual information requires an insert shot so they see clearly what is important, other times, simply bringing the camera closer to the action or changing the angle is all that is required to clarify the importance of the moment.

Logging the Takes

Once you have completed your photographic stage of your production, it is important to log the raw footage into its various elements, such as wide shots, close ups, background shots and so on. This gives you an opportunity to judge what  you have recorded before beginning the editing session. At this point you may decide that more shooting is required. It is best to discover that now rather than half way through the edit session.

If your editing software has the capability to show exact time code of each video frame or a reference frame number, you will be able to log exact locations for your raw footage you shoot.

Two popular edit software systems are Apple's Final Cut Pro (FCP) and Sony's Vegas Pro 10 (or higher). Both have an easy to follow time line for drag and dropping your raw footage to the time line and changing the length of your footage.

If you are working with another person as a team, it might be advantageous to use an old film editors technique of logging your takes with the media's reference numbers of each take with a brief description of the shot or take.

Example of logging sheet for recording your footage of material shot

Project: *Duck Music Video*

Source# start stop Scene Description Remarks
Page 4 of 10

Duck 03 1.03.20 1.04.10 Single
duck swims from group Good to 3.40
Duck 03 1.04.12 1.06.14 Wide shot
of pond - sunset Good at end?
Duck 03 1.06.12 1.08.00 Wide shot
of 4 ducks - sunset Good at start +:45

[Media's code number from the camcorder]

For logging shots you do not need frame numbers (If you are using time code).

Always list the number of pages for this file. It will help you keep from losing valuable information by keeping all of it together. Staple or paperclip these pages together.

This amount of information will give you a quick idea of where to find the footage for which you are looking. And you will find that it is time well spent when you begin the edit session or need to use something from this media months later.

Teacher's Note: Students should be required to turn in their log sheets with their finished video production to verify that proper logs were generated.

Chapter Three

Camera Techniques

Chapter One was an outline and an overview of some of the aspects of video production. In this chapter we will look at some camera techniques involved in video production. With the advent of constant changes in video formats and capabilities of the cameras with more and more ease of operation, it is not within the scope of this text to discuss the various formats and camera options available. Instead, we will focus on proficient camera practices in capturing images for your projects.

To record an image on your camcorder, there must be sufficient light, a degree of focus and proper framing. Otherwise your work will not be indistinguishable from your Great Aunt Mabel's camera work who has never owned a camcorder. You know the footage she shot at the last family reunion, everyone around the dinning table was in silhouette; most of everybody's head was cropped off and the focus seem to be on the tree outside the dinning room window, remember? Having everyone wave at the camera was an especially artist directional touch on her part as well, don't you think?

It can be convenient to have a camera do a lot of the thinking for you, if you are Aunt Mabel, but for professional productions you need to make lighting, focus and picture framing based on solid "Hollywood" techniques.

Lighting Techniques

In a later chapter we will discuss three point lighting, for now, you should at least be aware that your subject matter should be the brightest thing in the frame. Often with video, the light in the background is brighter than the face of your subject. In which case, the camera's electronics  balances the light exposure to that background amount of light. Your subject looks like they are in the witness protection program.

To avoid this silhouette effect, move the camera so that the bright light in the background is framed out of the picture. If that is not possible, you're only other choice is to light the face so that it is lighter than the background or manually over expose the background so that the face looks normal. Not a desirable situation, so if additional lighting is not practical, changing locations may be necessary. A good rule from the still photography  business is to try to stage your action so that the sun is over your shoulder, lighting your subjects naturally. In location scouting for this camera angle, being sensitive to these potential lighting and exposure problems in advance is an important part of your pre-production.

Proper Focus and Framing

We have all become lazy thanks to the introduction of the zoom lens. Instead of carefully staging setups with a fixed lens  camera, we stand in one place and zoom the camera in and out until our audience begins to get motion sickness. The zoom lens is a great tool when used properly. The proper procedure for setting the focus with a zoom lens is to zoom in all the way to the closest shot, set the focus and then zoom back out until the desired framing is achieved. This technique assures that the focus will be sharp for all focal planes of the zoom range. If you try to set focus zoomed out to the wide shot, should you zoom in at any time during your shot, the lens will go out of focus as the zoom closes in on the subject. The best use of the zoom lens on the camcorder is to adjust the framing size without having to move the camera tripod or camera person's position. Your productions will have a much more professional look if you keep your fingers off the zoom control while shooting. Leave that for Aunt Mabel. In a later chapter we will discuss the details of proper framing and picture composition, for now there are some simple rules that will help your presentations look more professional from the start. Although most of this is common sense and maybe things you already know, let's take just a moment to clarify some basics.

When photographing a person's face in a general or medium shot which is usually a head and shoulder shot, there are three basic directions the face can be pointing. Left profile, straight on and right profile or anywhere in between. If you imagine a line drawn down the center of the picture in the straight on shot, that line would run down the center of the actor's nose. Now, what happens if the actor turns left or right? If you pan the camera so that the imaginary line is still at the tip of the actor's nose and still close to the center of the screen, your picture will have just about the proper balance. This is not a hard fast rule, but it is a good general rule for creating the right balance. In short, you need to give the picture's framing some "breathing room" in front of the actor's face. If the actor is looking right frame and you place the actor's nose right at the edge of the right frame it would look badly composed, right? [See Illustrations]

Using the subject's nose as a guide for centering the picture composition

Too Right Framed   Off Centered to the Left   Too Left Framed

So if you remember to put the nose somewhere close to the center of the picture regardless of where the actor is looking, the composition will look about right.

Too much headroom above the actor's head looks strange and unprofessional and not enough headroom annoys the audience. Just a little clearance above the actor's head seems to look about right. If you watch live television programs you will see that professional camera people strive to compose their picture framing about there. Some modern films, in an effort to be "artsy", get away from this general rule, but if you study films of the forties and fifties you will see they follow this technique closely.

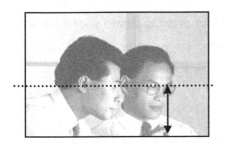 

Too Much Headroom **Not Enough Headroom**

Eye line too low Eye line too high

Correct Headroom For This Composition:

Eye Line Top Third of Picture

A final word about camera exposure. The high tech camcorder can record amazing pictures in almost no light, but that does not mean you should throw away your lighting package. The video camcorder has been a wonderful addition to our world, not the least of which is to allow you to learn the art of filmmaking without the expense and technical expertise required for film. For that we should all be thankful, but we should not assume that the camcorder has released us from proper lighting and proper exposure of the camera. What you get when you use these modern marvels of image capture without the proper amount of light is "grain" or more accurately in the video world, video noise. That immediately labels your work as amateurish. Bring the exposure index up with the right amount of light and your work looks more like the pros using film.

Example Assignment

Set up the camera and tripod for hands-on lab test of the various options available to you with your school's equipment. You should test the manual and auto exposure in different lighting situations, zoom control, focus control, and various framing compositions.

Teacher's Note: At this point, the school's camcorder(s) should be set up and it's operation be explained and demonstrated to the students, followed by a hands-on practice by each student.

Chapter Four

Learning to Think Like a Pro

Now that you have had some hands on experience with your camcorder and you are anxious to begin shooting, you should take a moment to consider the basic function the camera must perform. As you determine what the camera will record, first decide your interpretation of the subject of the video, and how you may suggest that thought to your audience. In order for your viewer to become involved in your video mentally and emotionally, you must use visual symbols that communicate the meaning you hope to express. For this to happen, you must control the attention of your audience to convey the mood of the scene, and establish an emotional environment. The way the camera is used will allow your audience to see, comprehend and be affected by those symbols. It is important not to allow your camera technique to distract the audience from that attention. Being clever with a camera only calls attention to it and therefore fragments the meaning you hope to express.

Mimicking Our Own Visual System

In the real world, our visual system of eyes and brain do amazing things for us that we never realize. We are walking along the sidewalk and we see a friend's car drive by. Without realizing it, we "zoom" into the car and see if our friend is driving and who might be with that person. All the while, our eyes are seeing the car, the street, and the trees on the other side of the street and so on. Our brain takes in all of this visual information, momentarily dismisses all else, and focuses only on our friend's face. As you read this text, your eyes see the whole page, your brain (zooms) sees only this line that you are now reading. As a filmmaker, your job with the camera is to determine what the audience's eyes should be focused on at any given time. This is done through the use of the camera angle and framing size of the shot. In the last chapter we learned the various general camera angles, such as the wide shot, medium shot and the close up. Now we will consider when and where those are important.

Camera Angles and Framing Techniques

Without realizing it, our brains have been making those decisions all of our lives. We are not even aware that it is happening. So an important way of deciding how much we want our audience to see is to become aware of just how our brains are doing that on a minute to minute basis. By controlling how much or how little we allow the audience to see through the use of the camera angle and framing, we control the audience's attention. That is something only you can decide, based on the story you are trying to tell to your audience.

As a general rule, television viewing is on a smaller screen than a movie theatre so you want to come in a little closer to your subject in all of your camera choices, so that it will not be too small to see on a small TV screen. The camera is the audience as a *spectator* to your action so where you place the camera for that action has an impact on the audience. If you want to convey the emotional aspect of a small child speaking to an intimidating adult, you might place the camera high, tilting down on the child, making the child look even smaller. The camera angle from the child's point of view (P.O.V.) tilting up to exaggerate the overpowering size of the adult. This is called the *subjective* use of the camera or a subjective angle. And it has an impact, emotionally.

Subjective Point of view – looking up

The "spectator" must be placed in a *possiblo* position, not a contrived one. Placing the camera inside a fireplace to view the scene outside a fireplace, through the flames, is not a possible position unless you want to be toasted. It will signal an unreal situation to your audience on a subconscious level.

When you place the camera just outside the action, so that your spectator is an invisible observer, it is considered and *objective* angle. Most of the camera angles you will probably use will be objective angles, with subjective angles used to make a point to your audience or direct their attention to the emotion that you want to convey.

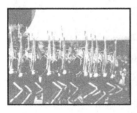

Three Examples of Objective Camera Angles

If you have a scene sequence that involves an exciting motorcycle race, cutting to the driver's P.O.V. so that the audience understands just how dangerous the action is, would be an example of using that subjective angle to express an emotion.

A person standing on a high ledge looking down, and suddenly cutting to a P.O.V. of the person and the seeing how far down the ground is below them will certainly convey an

emotion to the audience. An unexpected cut from an objective angle to a subjective angle can have shock value and impact on your audience, so you want to be sure that is what you want before using this technique. The camera angle involves a number of choices for you to make. The angle at which the scene is viewed, the size of the frame, and the height at which the camera is placed.

Viewing Angle

As mentioned previously, filmmaking transfers three dimensional space into the two dimensional space of the screen, so in order to give your audience a sense of the real world, you want to create a depth to your subject by seeing two sides and whenever possible the top or bottom of the subject. For example, seeing a box on a table from straight on gives a flat appearance, with no depth. By moving the camera slightly to toward one side so that two sides are seen, gives a feeling of depth to the box and by raising the camera angle toward the top of the box so that the top is also partially seen, creates a greater sense of reality.

Camera Height

An often neglected factor is the impact of what height at which the camera is placed has on the viewing audience. Usually, the placement of the camera is based on what is comfortable for the operator rather than the importance of that height to the audience in determining its reaction and emotional involvement in the video.

When shooting at a level angle the camera is placed at the eye level of the subject or the average height of most people. Always use the eye level of the subject being photographed whether standing or sitting, not the eye level of the operator or normal tripod height. If the subject is sitting, the camera angle should be lowered to match this level. Otherwise your camera angle becomes subjective by pointing the camera down on the subject.

Subjective angle of a base ball game

Deciding on Camera Angles

There are other considerations when deciding on high angle shots as related to covering the action from a distance or exteriors. For example, consider the following two angles. The first is the coverage of a football game from the announcer's booth that sees all of the field below. The second is on the sidelines of the field with the lens zoomed in on the players as they run the play. In the first angle, the camera can be locked down to a static shot that covers all of the action. The action seems slowed down because we see the player run without ever running out of frame. In the second, we must pan the camera to keep up with the action, we are in close and the scene seems much more dramatic because of the movement. There are reasons and considerations for the use of both angles. One slows the action down and conveys a sense of scale, the other creates emotion and excitement. How and when you use either shot conveys emotion and understanding to your audience on a subconscious level whether you realize it or not. Well, so much for the notion of *just point and shoot* your camcorder advertised on the box, huh?

Okay, so it is a little more complicated than you expected, but these are not tough decisions for you to make, or difficult concepts for you to understand, they are only aspects to be aware of as you plan where to place the camera before you shoot. With a little practice, it will all become second nature and after editing some of your first projects you will begin to make better judgments on camera placement and its impact on your audience. These are just secrets the pros use everyday in the films you enjoy watching and they add pleasure to your viewing because they took the time to consider the impact it would have on you. Now you can do the same for your audiences. Think like a pro. Be a pro.

Teacher's Note: At this point, the school's camcorder(s) should be set up and demonstrate examples of the text decision just made for the students, followed by hands on practice by each student.

Chapter Five

Your First Production

The process of making a film is complicated enough without the added burden of working with actors on your first project. For that reason, it is much easier to learn the camera placement and dynamics of the video frame by working by yourself. Your first project should be a music video where you conceive the types of shots you think would be suitable in telling your music video story without the use of actors. As dull as that might sound, your hands will be full just finding the right shots and how to use those shots in telling the story. Later, after you have some experience working with the camera and related equipment, you will be better suited to direct actors in telling a video story. Just as you would not want to have your first driving lesson including a car load of your friends, so you do not want your first project experience to include those added complications and pressures. If your facility has the capability, a good first project is to collect pictures and transfer those video files to the editing system, if not, then another tried and true method is to transfer actual pictures to video by way of an art stand. An art stand is a camera mounted vertically to photograph art work that is lighted from both sides. [See illustration next page] After the video has been put into the media storage device, your music can be laid down on your master, followed by cutting the pictures to match key points in the music score. As stated before, the music must always be edited first and then the pictures.

Video Art Stand

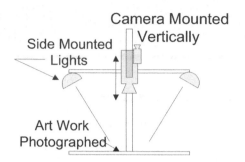

Camera Mounted
Vertically

Side Mounted
Lights

Art Work
Photographed

Student Critiques

Once all the student projects have been completed and screened for the entire class without comment or interruption, it is time for a second screening for the class with a critique by the fellow class members on each student's production. Although anyone's program can be picked apart by even well meaning critics, the best plan of action is to limit that criticism to positive comments that will help the filmmaker in future productions. What is most important at this stage is to understand the language of film and learn to "speak" it so that your audience can follow what you are trying to tell them. What you need to know is if they understand what the filmmaker was trying to tell them. If not, then they can say they didn't get what you were trying to show them. The following sentence probably should be in all caps, underlined and in bold type: Any good cinematic story can be told without <u>one</u> line of dialogue or voice over or most of all, narration. If you can remember that one thought and strive to tell your story on screen without the aid of dialogue, imagine how much impact your films will have *with* dialogue. Do that and you will be much better than most big name Hollywood directors and writers. Nothing kills a story quicker than a boring narration in the leading character's voice in the first frame of a film. It is like a giant disclaimer on the screen that reads: I have no idea how to show this story in pictures so I will just narrate what the actor is thinking.

Boring!

Don't do it. Learn to tell your story in pictures with emotions that come from camera angles and positions, with lighting and more important, shadows, with sounds that evoke emotional feelings, and settings that clarify your point of view. Then add the dialogue and your stories come to life on the screen and compel your audiences to take notice of your ability to communicate to their inner being. Yank them out of their seats and pull them onto the screen with you. As a young lad, I saw an episode of *Seventy Seven Sunset Strip* (Long before your time) called *The Silent Caper*, it was a special episode in which there was no dialogue for the entire hour program. Oh, there may have been one or two lines somewhere in the story, I don't remember. The story was about the guest star being kidnapped and held hostage. That aired in the early sixties and yet I still remember it, why? It was compelling *because* it had **no** dialogue. That impact on me was made long before I discovered I wanted to make movies.

A good second assignment would be to tell a short story without dialogue by just using cinematic elements to communicate your story to your audience and then have the other class members see if they can understand your story.

The third assignment should be to go back and re-shoot or re-edit the second assignment with the suggestions in mind that your classmates made on the second assignment's screening. By reworking a project instead of giving up and moving on, you learn both patience and resolve for seeing a project all the way to the end. Something professional filmmakers are doing right now, somewhere in some dark editing rooms, or in front of word processors, fixing multi-million dollar films that did not tell the audience the story they should have told. Take a straw poll of those people and you will no doubt discover that they never went to film school or took a class like the one your in now. So take heart, you will not make those mistakes as they have because you are learning your craft the right way. As a result, you will be much better prepared to be successful, should you choose to make this a lifelong career.

Picture Composition

Now that you have had some hands-on experience with the camera and created your first project, you no doubt have discovered that you have more questions. Just pointing the camera in the general direction of your subject is no longer good enough. Deciding on just the right framing, the best angle and the most  appropriate lighting has now become important to you. Congratulations, you are becoming an artist. In the last chapter we discussed angles, framing and the camera in a simplistic way so that you could get started with your first project. Like learning to ride a bicycle before learning to ride a Harley motorcycle, you are ready to look deeper into the subject of picture composition.

Composing a picture is made up of several elements. It is where you place the camera, at what height, what lens focal length, and what you frame the picture to include or exclude. These considerations determine whether your shot is objective or subjective, and if we include lighting into this equation, the *mood* of the shot. Lighting is such an important part of filmmaking that we will devote a whole chapter on the various aspects of three point lighting for film (or video), and It adds complications to this level of understanding. So we will add that to our equation later, for now let us look at the placement of the camera in deciding on our picture composition.

Camera Angles

One of the most important aspects of picture composition is the camera angle as it determines what our audience will view of the action. On another level there is the psychological and emotional

significance in the placement of the camera angle. The camera placed low and looking up at a subject on the screen can make the subject appear imposing. Placing the camera high, looking down on a character can make them look insignificant. Camera angles help the audience understand the subject we are presenting in more than just informational comprehension. The filmmaker should keep in mind that it is an important tool that should be used wisely to express the filmmaker's interpretation of the real world. Misplaced camera angles can send the wrong message to the audience or one that was not intended, which can dampen the effectiveness of the presentation.

Framing

As with a painter or a photographer, the frame is an important element in the cinematic expression by focusing the audience on only what the filmmaker wishes the audience to see. Usually, the focus of the action takes place in the frame of the picture, or  by deliberately excluding the action from the frame, the audience's attention or curiosity can be heightened. By having the action take place just beyond the frame line, the audience's anxiety is increased as they wonder what is happening. When the camera is panned or the angle changed to show the off-camera action, the anxiety is resolved. The filmmaker has created suspense.

Another consideration in framing your shots is the use of oblique framing. The camera is placed at an off level angle so that when viewed the image on the screen is off level that can serve to transmit more information to the audience about a character's condition. Is he drunk or crazy?

Unfortunately, the technique has been over used by wannabe MTV type directors for no reason and only confuses the audience rather than clarify a subjective emotion or mental condition. Don't break the rules unless you know the rules.

Example of Oblique Framing

By the use of objective (and/or oblique) framing and subjective angles, the filmmaker can allow the audience to view the world through the eyes of the character and evoke emotions through their involvement with the action. Utilizing these fundamental techniques, the filmmaker has the ability to do more than present an external view of the subject, the filmmaker can express the inner nature of the character.

Understanding the Lens

The advent of the sophisticated and complex camcorder has simplified the need for the filmmaker's understanding of the workings of the modern zoom and fixed focus lens. As a matter of fact, few  camcorders even allow you to remove the zoom lens and replace it with a fixed focus lens. For that reason, we will discuss the zoom lens only briefly in this text and those who have an interest may seek out more information on the net, a copy of *American Cinematographer Manual*, or your local library.

On major Hollywood productions where film cameras such as the Arriflex BL 35MM or Panaflex 35MM, which can cost as much as a small single family home are used, the importance of the lens is much greater. The three areas of importance of a lens are: Focus, depth of field, and the zoom capability. Other than the cardboard box cameras you pick up at the drugstore, all lens must have their focus set for the subject to be in focus. The depth of field is the area in front of the camera that is in relative focus. An example would be to focus on a subject that is say, three feet in front of the camera. If the subject moves a little closer or slightly back, they will still *appear* to be in focus. Once they move too far in either direction their image will appear to go soft or out of focus. So it can be said that the focus has been set for a depth of field that is three feet in front of the camera. Professional filmmakers will often use a tape measure from the camera to the subject to insure that the proper focus has been set, since their eyes may not be perfect when looking through the viewfinder. It may seem overly cautious but when considering how the film will be projected onto a large theatre screen, and every detail blown up so large, it is not worth taking a chance. So the depth of field of a lens is the distance from the nearest and farthest point within which the subject will be in *acceptable* sharpness when the lens is set at less than infinity.

Zooming Along

As stated previously, the proper way to set the focus on a zoom lens is to zoom in all the way on a subject and adjust the focus on the face, a button on the clothing, a nametag or the camera slate. Then, as you zoom back out, everything in that depth of field will be in focus. If you do not zoom all the way in before setting the focus, you will find if you change the frame size by zooming in or out, that you were not really in focus.

The zoom mechanism itself was created to serve two key needs of the camera person. One, to allow different framing sizes without changing a fixed lens or the distance from the camera to the subject, and two, to allow the camera person to follow changing action by altering the framing size *on the fly*. Live coverage of sporting events, ice skating, and awards shows are good examples of the use of the zoom lens zooming on the fly. As professional as all of those uses are, for you to use a zoom during your productions will make it look less professional. During the seventies when the zoom lens was first thought of as an acceptable addition to the filmmaker's resources, there was a rush of films that all used "live" zooms to cover the action. Be glad it was before your time, it was very annoying because it was used more as a gimmick than an invisible technique. Should you watch some of those films or catch an old episode of the original *Mission Impossible* or *Mannix*, you will see their use of the live zoom.

Long Lens, Wide Angle Lens
The 'long lens' can either be a separate lens that is attached to the camera for a special shot or it can be the zoom lens zoomed all the way in and used to bring something very distant up close. A set of binoculars is in effect a long lens, as is a telescope. The wide angle lens is just the opposite. When the zoom lens of the camcorder is zoomed all the way back to the largest field of view, it is considered wide angle. A fisheye lens or setting on a zoom lens is this widest angle.

Wide Angle Lens	**Long Lens**
Notice how the buildings look like they are bowing out from the center of the picture.	Notice the flattening of the opera house against the buildings of the city beyond

A good example of the ultimate fisheye lens is the peephole in a front door that shows an ultra wide view of someone at the front door of an apartment or home. The lowest millimeter reading on the lens is the widest angle and the highest reading is the longest angle. In 35MM film cameras a normal lens (Most like the human eye) is 35MM, lower than that becomes a wider angle. Longer lens in 35MM begin around 70MM, with 135MM + used as a telescope point of view simulation. In 16MM those previous numbers would be divided roughly in half. Your camcorder would probably be halved again, depending on the size of the CCD image collector. Long lens tend to flatten objects in the frame out, where as wide angle lens tend to exaggerate the curve of the shape. You probably have seen that exaggeration in a comic scene at some time.

Class Exercise

At this point set up the camera and demonstrate how the zoom lens works, the effect of setting focus the proper way and then the incorrect way (zoomed out) to show how misleading that can be. Then experiment with shooting subjects at various distances from the camera to discover the impact of *depth of field*.

And finally, experiment with framing sizes and the difference of long lens and wide angle lens positions.

Chapter Six

Editing Your Projects

In every aspect of our lives we have rules that we must follow. There are rules for safely operating a power saw or a motor vehicle. If we break these rules we create problems for ourselves. In the creative world there seems to be a notion that it is okay, if not desirable, to "break the rules". Nothing could be farther from the truth. It is one of the great myths of the creative world. On close examination you will discover that the great artists that 'broke all the rules' had in fact, at the heart of their craft, a strict adherence to the rules. How they *applied* those rules is from whence the genius came.

Making the Right Cut

As with any artistic and creative endeavor, editing has certain rules that should always be followed. The ease of non-linear editing has made it possible for anyone to edit video. Unfortunately,  the software that comes with those systems does not include warning labels or instructions on how to make proper edits. Like a monkey banging on a piano, it's not music coming out of the piano, it is only sounds that are unrelated and follow no theme or pattern and certainly no rhythm. MTV was probably the most likely source for the total destruction of learning the importance of "playing music" instead of "monkeys banging on pianos". The reason was simple.

Recording artist in the eighties were too cheap to pay for real editors to turn out quality work. So uneducated, wannabe 'editors' banged on visual pianos until young people thought it was visual music. It became a style and it is far too late to convince young people otherwise. The good news is that it is largely self contained and if you have no interest in learning the rules there is a venue where you can bang on a piano all you want.

If you like MTV/VH1 and that style of nonsense edits you will be wasting your time to read on. On the other hand, if you have watched MTV and lately decided you are outgrowing it, you are beginning to realize that maybe it is possible to play real 'music' in your world of editing, and you are ready to open the door to something that will greatly broaden your horizons and give you the missing key to beautiful and invisible editing.

It is All About Rhythm

If you read books by seasoned film editors or if you are lucky, and run across an interview with one, you will eventually hear the term: **Rhythm**. The rhythm of editing. How do you know what that is, how do you learn how to have rhythm in your editing and how do you know when it is missing or off?

The answer is both simple and complex. Untrained singers often sing off key and they don't know it. Others hear them and find it grading on their nerves. Some singers go through life singing off key and torturing their friends and love ones. Your editing will be just as off key if you do not take the time to learn the rhythm of editing. One of the best ways to learn editing is cutting a music video. It contains all the necessary nutrients for building strong and healthy editing habits. It has inherent rhythm, it has a story to tell, and it is the easiest editing to do. It is a perfect place for beginners to start to learn.

Let's go back to our illustration of the singer singing off key. They don't know they are off key, would be embarrassed if they realized it and would be grateful if someone would help them correct it. They should not be ridiculed for not knowing because they can't help it. As long as they are singing to a group of tone deaf listeners they may never have their problem discovered. On the other hand, if they have any hope of singing in front of professional musicians they better get help. Assuming you want to have your editing work seen by the rest of the world, then you want to learn to edit in rhythm and on key.

If you think about a small group of musicians forming a band or a rock group which hopes to perform their own compositions, then it would be logical to assume that even if they did not know how to write their music down in the proper sheet music form, they could at least have some plan to follow each other. If one is on a piano, another is on bass guitar and another in on drums, how do they decide how long to hold a note before playing the next? The answer is, that critical timing comes from the drummer. The beat of the drum. That rhythm cues the other players where they are, in the overall timing of the music. So in its simplest terms, the beat sets the pace and governs the timing.

Cutting on the Beat

Editing must adhere to a beat, a rhythm. Music especially must be edited by cutting *on* the beat. How do you cut *on* the beat? It helps to be able to read music, if not, at least understand how it is written down on paper.

The smallest division is the note; the next division that most laymen can see or hear is the bar. That is as far as we need to understand for now. Music, as it relates to editing on video can be thought of in terms of beats per minute. Some techno music runs in the range of 128 beats per minute or two beats per second. Classical music runs at the other end of the spectrum. Rock music runs somewhere in between. From 60 to 96 beats per minute. Most of the software programs have this information on their visual timeline, which makes your job pretty much a no-brainer.

In a slow paced classical music video, hard cuts look too abrupt. Dissolves or soft cuts seem to flow much better. In rock music a dissolve seems out of place for the same reason. If you are not aware of an editing secret call the *soft cut,* it is a two to four frame dissolve. It is important to understand how to cut on the beat from a theory standpoint so we will first explain that and then explain an easy way to accomplish it with a very simple rule that takes all the math out of it.

Developing a Sense of Timing

If your sense of timing is so bad you can't possibly ever hope to clap in time with the music or hear the beat as you edit. You might want to think about some other endeavor. If not, then again, the software can help. On the timeline you will see the visual representation of the drumbeat or the guitar strum or some other indication that a note has been played. It has a time code location, frame number or fraction of a second and it will appear on the timeline in exact repetitions. You do not make a cut in the middle of one of these notes; you make the cut just as the sound of the note happens. Now, due to the visual timing and reproduction of the images, by the time that appears on the screen It may appear out of sync. So you must adjust the cut so that it appears in sync and on the beat. Whatever that delay, if any, would be followed for the duration of the piece and in fact probably everything you cut on that system of software. For example: adjust by plus or minus one or two frames.

So the first unbreakable rule is you **never cut any picture except on the beat**.

When do you cut, how often and where are all questions easily answered by the music itself. The easy way to figure that out is to cut at the end of a bar of music if your ear can hear that group of notes. If not, then listen to the singer in the music for the end of that phrase, for example the phrase might be: "I only want to be with you." Maybe that is a reoccurring phrase. If you cut away to the next shot on say the word "want" or at different words in that phrase throughout the song, your editing will look amateurish. If you make all your cuts on "you". Then your editing will not put off people with professional understanding. You won't be "out of key".

So the second unbreakable rule is that you **only cut at the end of a bar or phrase of music**.

As you assemble the footage for the video you will see certain visual elements that tie into the music. An easy example might be a runner running. It should not be too much of a stretch to realize that as the runner's foot hits the track is the exact moment that should be in sync with the beat of the drums or the beat of the music. As obvious as that is when you think about it, most beginning editors never realize that is where it should happen. Another example might be footage of waves crashing on the rocks. As the waves break and splash, should be in-sync with the beat of the music. These are subtleties that professional editors build into their work that gives it a rhythm that the audience without realizing it, picks up on and judges the work to be above average rather than ordinary.

Finer Points of Timing

In cutting music videos, there are moments with each shot that also fit the beat or they are out of sync with the beat. Let's use the example of a country western video where we see the actor standing at a refrigerator as she  closes the door. There are a number of ways to determine when the cut should occur; all of which depend on the action itself. If the scene should finish with the closing of the door, the beat will occur as the door closes creating the effect of the sound of the door shutting being the downbeat of the drum. If the cut is two seconds in length, then you would back time the cut from the door shut to wherever you are two seconds prior. If the action calls for you to see the actor just after the door closes for some reason, then you still want the "sound" of the door shut to be with the beat of the drum, only not the down beat. If there are aspects of the front of the shot having to be some exact moment, say in order to be in sync with a previous shot, then you solve this problem by adjusting the timeline. Let's say from the head of the shot to the door close is at one and three-quarter seconds instead of your needed two full seconds. By stretching the shot to two seconds both the head of the shot occur at the right moment and the in-sync moment occur at the proper place. Most software has some way of tweaking the timeline. In the old days we used a playback machine with slo-mo capability.

In its most elemental division, music videos are divided into beats per minute. If you are editing amateur music this may turn out to be inconsistent and chaotic when analyzed on your computer's software timeline. With professional music (Or amateur music using a drum synthesizer) this will be consistent. And since it is, you will discover that these beats neatly fall into segments of one, two (not often three) four, six and eight seconds. This makes you job much easier because you now have a easy pattern to follow that makes you look like an experienced editor that understands rhythm. You cut on one, two, three or four second intervals. Of course if it is at the chorus you might have some reason to hold the shot for eight seconds. Usually not.

The third unbreakable rule is you **only make cuts on one, two, three or four seconds intervals**.

Let's say you decide not to follow this rule. You make one cut at one and a half seconds and the next at two and three quarter seconds bringing you into the next edit at four and one half seconds. You are now a half a beat out of sync, if you continue to do this, your work will look chaotic and unprofessional on a subconscious level.

"Did you like my video?" "No, it graded on my nerves, but I couldn't tell you why."

It is all about rhythm.

Can you ever break these rules? My old standby is you should not break the rules unless you know the rules. How does that apply here?

For some reason in your edited piece you have the need to hold the shot a few frames longer, usually because the timeline can not be altered without some noticeable problem or you must keep in lip-sync. So you hold that shot the needed few extra frames knowing that you are breaking a rule. You get out of this by making up for it on the next shot. Maybe you shorten it so that you are back on the one, two, three, or four rhythm. Maybe you can't make up for it on the next shot so you hold that one longer until you get back in sync. There are any number of ways around these situations, the important thing to remember is to get back on track as soon as possible (And do not try to start a "new" rhythm.).

I have used the example of one, two three and four-second shots. In practice, the one-second shot is quite annoying to the viewer and should be avoided if at all possible. Keep in mind that you have looked at this footage over and over and know what it says visually. Your audience has not seen it. They will see it one time. There is too much visual information on one second of footage for people to digest. Two seconds is a bare minimum. If you are cutting techno music you may get by with it, but it makes itself aware of itself to the audience. Editing should always be <u>invisible</u>.

Now that you understand rhythm, you will start to see it in everything you watch (except maybe MTV/VH1). Whether it is a musical number on an awards program or a music video on Country Music Television (CMT), you will see that most of the cuts are on a two or four or six-second interval following a time tested pattern. You may or may not care for the type of music you see and hear on CMT but without question the money that is spent on those videos reflect the quality and taste of not beginners who do not know what they are doing but true professionals who have honed their skills from countless hours sitting in dark edit bays listening to the beat of the music and making their cuts with style and rhythm. A good way to learn editing is to spend some time watching CMT videos. Faith Hill probably has the most artistic and professional videos in the business. I would judge them to be in excess of one half million dollars each. You don't entrust that kind of money on wannabe editors.

With any rule there are exceptions. Of late I have noticed that certain editors on CMT have begun cutting one word before the end of the bar or phrase. Perhaps they think they are *leading* the cut to the next action, I don't know. Perhaps they are hoping to create some new trend. Trends come and go, eventually fading for the simple reason they call attention to the editing and that never lasts for too long.

As you graduate to cutting dialogue in dramatic scenes you will discover that it too has a rhythm. This rhythm is derived from the pace of the dialogue and the action associated with it. An intimate scene between two characters with fast cuts looks unprofessional. A heated argument between several people at odds with each other looks equally unprofessional with long takes on one actor who is no longer talking. It becomes a matter of keeping up with the action. It is okay and usually desirable to hold on the key character while another speaks off camera, especially if it is a brief word and then the key character has another long line of dialogue. As you begin to learn the rhythm of editing, these situations will have the proper answer in the wide shot's pacing. Key your cutting to the pace the director set with the action itself. Everything else will fall into place and you will realize that the rhythm you learned in music videos has given you the understanding you needed to be able to cut dialogue scenes in feature style movies.

This is by no means all you need to know about rhythm. It is, I hope a starting place to a much bigger, more complex and sophisticated art form called editing. Like playing a piano, practice makes perfect. The more you strive to do better work, the more you will discover how best to do it. The more invisible your work will become, until you reach the point that when you ask others what they thought of your editing, they say the highest words of praise that you can get: "I didn't really <u>notice</u> the editing."

Cutting Techniques

Over the years I have been amazed at some of the ways other editors have attempted to edit music to picture. If you are working on a high budget feature film you might have the luxury of having a composer fit the music to your edited picture. For the rest of us who  must fit the picture to the *edited* music, there is only one way to accomplish this while cutting on the beat.

First, the music track is laid down in black, and then you lay down the wide shot of the performer. In the case of having the music "live" then that becomes an automatic one-pass procedure, that is, the track and wide shot are already together. You now have an overall performance of the music video. This is the point at which a MTV type editor says in his mind, I have no idea what to do next so I'll just start laying down shots and hope it looks like I know what I'm doing.

You *do* know what to do next. Looking at your "trim bin"(logged shots) you find a lip-sync match point for the first close-up of the performer if that is the style of your piece or you find the first cut of your storyline to be inserted. This edit point should be at a point that feels comfortable to ease into the second shot. In filmmaking parlance the first shot is the establishing shot, meaning you are telling your audience where you are. Live concert, country road, Skateboard Park. The second shot Is the character establishing shot. In other words, let the audience get to know what the central character looks like.

If your storyline has some tie-in with the song itself, the procedure is a simple act of matching the lyrics to the action and cutting that into the wide shot performance as needed using your technique of cutting on the end of a bar of music or phrase. Using the example above: "I only want to be with you". You obviously want to show the audience examples of that feeling. That can be as unique as someone doing outrageous acts in order to be with that person. So when we hear that lyric we expect to see an example of that feeling. This is your theme. If your storyline has to do with an object instead of a person then you want to treat that object as a person. It becomes your central character.

Maybe it's a racecar or a skateboard. The second shot might be the close-up of the wheels of the skateboard as the rider checks the race (ball bearings) in the wheels. The music is fast paced so we want quick action shots to build the drama. The board hits the ground, P.O.V. shots from a camera mounted on the front of the board as the exciting down hill run begins. Your theme could very easily be the P.O.V. camera. Skateboarding is about movement so the camera wants to move with the action, you want to intensify that action. There is a dangerous ramp up ahead. Show how dangerous that ramp is by cutting away to a close-up with a fisheye lens to exaggerate the leap. Then back to the action. Will he make this jump?

What are you doing?

You are building drama into your music video. People want to see drama, whether that is conflict between people or the conflict of whether or not the skateboarder will make the big jump. If you are not cutting to build the action to a final resolve you are not cutting like a genuine editor, you are just playing with some really cool toys. And that too is fine if that is all you want to accomplish. If you really like editing and want to do it, then think about:

1) What is my story in this piece?

2) How do I show it?

3) How do I 'sell' it to the audience?

4) How do I make it compelling and unique?

5) What is the climax of the important action?

6) How do I bring it to resolve?

7) Have I told a story that the audience will remember or are these just connected shots with no theme?

I am a strong believer in scripts, script outlines, and storyboarding. That is where you begin. It should be the first thing you do before the  video is shot and the last thing you put down when you finish editing your video. Computers make us lazy by doing a lot of work for us. Some systems log our shots and match the dialogue in filing the takes. I have yet to see a system that writes a storyboard or an outline. There really is no excuse for an editor not being organized and clear about the direction he or she wants to go in the journey from raw footage to edited master. You should work to see it on paper before you start, if you want to 'play music' instead of 'bang on a piano'. It still can be more fun than work.

Class Exercise

At this point set up the editing system that the students will be using and demonstrate how it works, the effect of the various functions that the equipment can perform and the proper way to begin the editing session.

Each student should then have a hands-on experience with several simple edits with the class observing.

Chapter Seven

On Screen Graphics

The alpha-numeric symbols electronically generated and placed on the screen of a video frame which give you additional information are often referred to as: "Graphics"

In connection with the last chapter on editing, the graphics that are placed on the screen for any number of reasons, should be discussed in regard to the picture composition as it relates to graphics on the screen.

Very often I see students who have not paid much attention to the television program graphics they have seen all their lives, place their graphics on the screen the same way they would if they were pasting up a magazine ad copy. That is, covering the entire screen from top to bottom. For that reason we will consider some basics about the proper placement of graphics on the screen for video and film production.

OUR VACATION
TRIP TO
BEAUTIFUL
NORWAY

The wrong way to place screen graphics

With the exception of opening or closing credits on a video production, the use of graphics should always be second to the importance of what else is on the screen. This is why the standard for graphic layout is to place these elements on what is called the lower thirds. If you divide the screen into vertical areas of three segments you will see that the bottom third is where you have always seen alpha-numeric symbols or the printed words.

This allows the viewer to process that graphic information as desired without losing the focus of what else is being broadcast visually.

Graphics placed in the lower third of the picture

The Cluttered Screen

In the mid-nineties, networks and later independents started placing a logo in one of the lower corners of the screen in what is referred to as embossed transparency. ABC and CBS did it with the most class, using a small circle symbol of their logos. NBC, having a spread peacock fan had theirs larger and of course they could not resist the temptation to do some advertising by placing the logo for the Olympic games below that. Which we need to see continuously lest in our enormous stupidity, we will forget that they are the broadcaster of it a year or two from now (Like we need that information right now). At the turn of the century, some middle management moron came up with the idea of placing advertising of up coming programming into that corner as well, in the same style as that annoying internet advertising to which we are constantly being subjected. *TV Guide* recently referred to this practice by giving it a name: "Clutter". Webster's dictionary describes clutter as being: *n*. A disordered state; jumble. *−v*. To litter.

Don't *litter* your screen.

Discovering the Character Generator

Students who are first discovering the character generator creating these words for the screen often fall into the trap of playing with the graphics on the screen. Indulging themselves with all the many font types and styles without understanding that for the public, these symbols have a history in meaning. For example, there is a font that looks like a group of wooden boards slapped together to form a letter. It looks unique but is difficult to read and has a universal meaning of country or western motif. A bar-be-queue restaurant might have such a font for their business sign. So being cute is not the best approach. The optimum approach is to keep in mind that the sole purpose of graphics on the screen is to convey information to the audience in the most straightforward way. This means using a font that is easy to read and can be reduced to a very small size on the screen without confusion. On word processors a font that meets this criteria is usually called "Ariel" which has no wings or additional curls such as a Times Roman type font.

Ariel   Times Roman

Within the frame of the video screen there is an area called the *safe action area* this is an imaginary frame area about ten percent smaller on each side, than the actual screen size. The reason for this is to make up for the cutting off of the edges of the screen through broadcast or reproduction in the VCR or DVD. So graphics want to be placed no closer than ten percent of the screen size for each side. This allows for a space of about eighty percent of the screen. Graphics outside this area will likely be cut off in transmission and will not be read by the viewer.

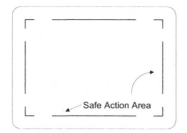

Standard Broadcast Frame   **HDTV Broadcast Frame**

There is a long ago accepted protocol of screen etiquette for placing graphics on the screen that you should be aware. These are not commandments but highly advised suggestions:

☐ Graphics should be placed as small as possible without being difficult to read.

☐ Graphics should be of the same size and font throughout the program.

☐ Graphics should be of a color and style that is easy to read over the background colors or images. Reds and oranges should be avoided.

☐ Graphics should appear on the screen long enough to be read twice by the average reader.

☐ Graphics should be used at a minimum if possible.

☐ Graphics should convey important information to the audience about the subject or the person appearing on camera.

☐ Graphics should be placed within the safe action area.

☐ Graphics should not jump around on the screen from cut to cut.

☐ Graphics should not be placed higher than the bottom third of the screen, and if at all possible, the bottom fifth of the screen.

☐ Graphics read left to right so left justified is preferred over center justify. Right justify should be avoided as it takes longer for the human eye to find to scan.

The exception to this rule includes the opening screen credits where a single name appears, especially when it appears over a black screen. Often in this case it is desired to place the credit in the center of the frame. Another exception would be when the graphics need to appear next to an image appearing on the screen that is not in the center. An example would be an advertisement for a product that appears on screen to one side with other objects appearing on screen at the same time.

Centered Graphic

The Latest

In Camera

Technology

Simple to Use

Just Point and *Click!*

Graphics Determined by Visual Elements

Class Exercise

In the video frame place a visual from several sources that have different backgrounds and colors. This should include people addressing the camera, landscapes of several types, and several background colors and/or textures. Use the character generator that you normally use in class to demonstrate various types and fonts that are normally used for class projects.

What is the effect on the following set of circumstances:

Landscape Background-

Joe College

Reporting Live From Palm Beach

- Font sizes
- Font colors
- Font positions on the screen

Non-descript textured or computer generated backgrounds

- Font sizes
- Font colors
- Font shapes

People appearing on camera

- Font sizes
- Font colors
- Font shapes
- Font positions on the screen

The impact of colors of fonts on top of background of similar colors should be discussed. The difficulty of legibility of fancy or busy fonts should be considered as well.

Chapter Eight

The Importance of Lighting

One of the most often ignored elements of filmmaking is lighting. We live in an age when it is so easy to let our magic boxes do our creative work for us. As a painter uses oil color to paint his canvas, so the filmmaker should use light to  paint his or her video canvas. During the golden age of Hollywood the speed of the film stock was much slower than today's high speed film, as a result, movie sets required much more light and the lights were not the bright halogen lights we use today. This created a situation where lighting was 'pooled' rather than flooded the whole set. That is why the films of the forties and early fifties had the wonderful mottling and shadows that are missing in today's features. Since most films were in black and white, the lack of color necessitated that style of lighting to bring more depth and perspective to their work. Now, we just flood the set with too much light or shoot with available light so all the actors look like they are in the witness protection program.

To be sure, lighting is one of the most important elements of creative filmmaking providing you with great latitude for creating emotion ranges. Low illumination to set a solemn, sad mood, bright illumination to establish a happy ambiance. With all the ranges in between for a variety of moods. These are called low-key and high key lighting. Before we get into the details of mood lighting, we must first examine how to generally light a basic set.

Three Point Lighting

The term, three point lighting comes from the use of three main lights used to light a subject. Within the confines of a large set where actors are moving about, it would be almost impossible to light the set with only three points of light. That is not what is meant by that term. It refers to how the individual actor is lit.

The strongest light in the three point lighting set up is the key light. The next is the fill light and the third light is what is often called the back light or 'kicker', as it kicks an additional amount of light on the back of the head and shoulders of the actor to separate them from the background.

The key Light

The key light is the main source of light on the actor's face and body. If you where shooting an exterior location, it would be the same as the sun. Think about how bright the sun is on a person's face on a cloudless day. Now imagine that they are wearing a baseball cap to shade their eyes. Now, what do you see? You see a heavy dark shadow under the bill of the cap shading their forehead and maybe their eyes. Our eyes, like the camera, "stops" down the iris in ours eyes (and camera) to expose the sunlight at the proper exposure. This means that everything in shadow becomes very dark by contrast. Thus the term contrast ratio. It is the ratio of dark to light or in this case, shadow to very bright. In the real world, the light of a bright sunny day bounces around in our world to create a certain amount of "fill" light so that even the shaded area of our face with the baseball cap example is lighted so that we can still see the person's eyes, plus our brains do a certain amount of exposure adjustment to compensate for the high contrast ratio of the light to dark situation. Using this illustration further, we can see that our light on the set needs a fill light to fill in those shaded areas. The ratio of these two lights, the key light and the fill light determine the mood of our lighting. Strong shadows where the key light is much brighter than the fill light, creates a somber dark mood. When the ratio between the two is low, meaning the two lights are close to the same intensity, the mood is lighter or more cheerful.

Horror films tend to have a high ratio between the key and fill lights. Comedies tend to have a low ratio between the two main sources of light.

Where the key light is placed is of utmost importance in professional lighting. The proper location is slightly off axis from the camera, pointing at the subject, on one side of the camera. On which side the key light is placed is determined by the motivation of the key light source. That will be explained in detail later. The closer the key light is placed to the camera, the less shadow of the actor will be seen in the background. If the camera operator complains that the key light is burning his or her ear, then consider the light to be in the proper location. Okay, move it away from their ear, if you must. The fill light should be placed on the opposite side of the camera from the key light to balance the hard shadow created by the key. The best placement is on a line about forty-five degrees from the key, in an arc toward the actor.

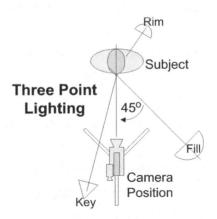

Three Point Lighting

[See Illustration]

Notice strong key light on left side of the face, and rim lighting highlighting the hairline and shoulders.

An Example of Three Point Lighting

Motivational Light Sources

Film and video lighting should compliment and enhance nature. After all, this is a creative field and you should strive to make your lighting look normal and yet something better than what is there. The question that immediately comes to mind when the director presents you with the location or set is: How do I light this? Unless you are using flashlights to view the location, the answer is right there in front of you. The light that makes it possible for you to see the set or location is coming from where?

There is a lamp on a desk in the corner. There is a fireplace and the scene calls for night (and it is not summertime), or there is a large window with sunlight coming in and the scene calls for late afternoon. These are all your natural sources of light. We call it your motivational source. Actors will sometimes ask a director: What is my motivation? Wanting to know why the actor would do thus and so. The Director of Photography or Cinematographer (as I think they should be called) can ask themselves the same question when it comes to wondering how to light the set. What is the motivation? Is it that sunlight coming in the window, or the lamp in the corner or even the light from the fireplace? Once the scene is blocked and you see where the action line is (180° rule) in the room, then you know where the key light should be located.

Example of strong motivational light source

For example, let us say that the action takes place so that the sunlight is coming in from your left (as the camera) and the actor's right side. You want the key light to be placed on the left side of the camera and therefore lighting the right side of the actor's face (as though it were the sun). That automatically puts the fill light on the right side of the camera, forty-five degrees off axis from the camera to light the left side of the actor's face for the fill source. All of that decision making took less than two seconds in your mind because you now know the right question to ask yourself when you arrive at the location. What is your motivational light source?

For another example, only this time, the scene calls for night so there is no sunlight. Look around the room and see what your light sources are for a natural look. A lamp on the desk and a fireplace. Great! The lamp is your key light source and the fireplace is your fill light source, not only that, but you get to put a warm gel on the fill light to approximate the warm glow of a fire or some pros put a dimmer on the fill so that it creates a more amber light. Dimming lights, gels and color temperature are all technical matters to be covered later.

The wave of horror films of the late seventies and early eighties stretched the term "motivational light source" to the max. The scenes would call for some poor girl running from the latest monster in a pitch black room or hall and yet we could see her face. Where did that light come from? Well, you can always fall back on the moon as a motivational light source, after all, monsters only come out on a full moon, and anyone knows that.

Back Lighting

The final light to consider in the three point lighting setup is the backlight or kicker light (or rim light). The purpose of this light is to separate the actor from blending into the background. This one light probably does more to separate the pros from the amateurs in its use. Watch any television newscast and look at the anchor's

shoulders and rim of their head and you will see the indication of the rim light. That light that points down from high above the anchor to light the back of their

Arrows Indicate Effect of Rim Light

head and shoulders creates a nice hard edge that is brighter than the news set background. Things which are lighter, appear closer to the camera, things which are darker, appear farther away. You need separation from the background in order to create a three dimensional depth in the two dimensional video and film frame. Where exactly should the rim light be placed?

No hard rule here, it is sometimes determined by the location possibilities and or problems. In general, if you can place it on the opposite side of the key light it will balance that strong source better than having it on the same side. In other words, if the key light is on the right side of the actor, then the kicker light should be hitting the left and rear side of the actor. The reason you place the light very high and to the rear of the actor is because if you place it low, there will be no rim effect on their head and shoulders.

Class Lab Assignment

At this point you should set up the three point lighting plan. View the results on a monitor for the entire class, followed by a discussion by class members. If at all possible, the room should be darkened so that only the three lights illuminate the subject for the camera.

Light Intensification

Now that we have an understanding of where to put the lights, we need to decide how much light to use for a proper exposure. This is a major problem for low budget, non theatrical films and video projects. The reason is the availability of the correct size lighting packages. One of the most popular and most affordable lighting packages are the Lowel Light kits. They have made it possible for low budget projects to shoot on location for years and their products are reasonably priced and well designed. Their standard halogen light is a five hundred watt and one thousand watt light. The one thousand watt light is generally referred to in the business as a one "K" (1K) light (1000 watts or 1 kilowatt). The typical three light kit of lights, stands and accessories provide a basic lighting package.

The problem with creative lighting using these basic systems is the amount of light they put out. If you use a 1K for a key light and five hundred watt light as your fill, you now have fifteen hundred watts of light in the room. If that is a room which is painted off white you can forget the term "mottling" when it comes to painting with light. That amount of light is equal to fifteen, one hundred watt light bulbs in one room. Lowel makes a VIP kit, which are much smaller lights that I have used and found to be a good solution to the problem of too much light on the set. The kits are easy to find at their web page. Another solution is to buy halogen work lights on stands at the Home Depot or hardware stores at a fraction of the price of the Lowel Light kits, however the stands do not have the height of the Lowel kits nor the scrim capabilities or accessories to flag, defuse and bounce the source light. (Terms that we will cover later.)

So the problem becomes how to get rid of all the light with which we just bombarded the set, in order to achieve a modeled, interesting look. If we can not bring the light level down, our actors will look like they are being "sweated out" in an interrogation room in cheesy foreign police station.

A popular light which you can buy for a few dollars is a 'par 16' halogen light in various wattages. A common wattage is fifty watts in either one hundred and twenty volt models or twelve volt models. To date, no manufacture that I am aware produces such a light on a stand for filmmakers (except for on camera battery powered lights), so you may have to create one if you are mechanically inclined, which I have done with great success, using parts commandeered from the lighting trade. [See illustration next page]

Remembering the look we mentioned earlier of the forties black and white films where pools of light were created because they did not bombard the whole set with light, then we can create that wonderful dramatic look by using smaller wattage lights sources. This has a two fold benefit. One, we decrease the electrical load on the outlets we are using, and two, we get a much more dramatic look, thanks to being able to add some shadows to the background and in some cases, the actor's face if the scene calls for that kind of look. Speaking of electrical loads-two Lowel Lights plugged into one outlet can trip an electrical breaker very quickly. Few directors enjoy having the lights go out in the middle of a perfect take, so you might want to spread that load out over more than one outlet. A good rule of thumb is to never plug two lights into one outlet.

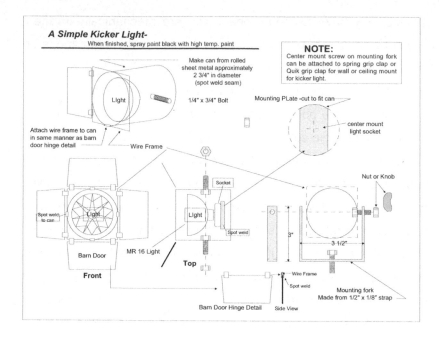

A Simple Kicker Light-
When finished, spray paint black with high temp. paint

Make can from rolled
sheet metal approximately
2 3/4" in diameter
(spot weld seam)

Light

1/4" x 3/4" Bolt

Mounting PLate -cut to fit can

Attach wire frame to can
in same manner as barn
door hinge detail

Wire Frame

center mount
light socket

NOTE:
Center mount screw on mounting fork
can be attached to spring grip clap or
Quik grip clap for wall or ceiling mount
for kicker light.

Socket

Nut or Knob

Spot weld
to can

Light

Light

Spot weld

3"

3 1/2"

Barn Door

MR 16 Light

Top

Front

Wire Frame

Spot weld

Mounting fork
Made from 1/2" x 1/8" strap

Barn Door Hinge Detail   Side View

Painting With Light

One of the nice things about cable television is they continue to recycle programs. One such example is *Unsolved Mysteries*. There are few examples better than *Unsolved Mysteries for* teaching lighting. The program re-enactment segments were shot in sixteen millimeter (16MM) and transferred to video tape for broadcast. Over the years there were no doubt different crews that did the lighting but it always had a consistent quality and style. For the cinema-graphically dull "talking heads" segments, the D.P. would often place a pink gelled light to sweep in one direction in the background, with a blue gelled light sweeping the background from the other direction. This created an effect that made one side of an object in the background look blue and the other pink. Since the light was also flagged with a 'cookie' that breaks up part of the light, it created a random pattern of blues and pinks. In the foreground there would be the proper exposure for the subject so this background effect remained subtle and yet visually interesting. If you are able to catch a rerun of the program, turn off the sound so that you can study the lighting design without the distraction of becoming interested in the story.

For a quick explanation of the terms 'cookie' and 'flag', think about a street light with a tree between the light and the sidewalk at night. The shadows falling on the sidewalk from the tree's foliage, creates both a flag and a cookie. The term cookie is short for cukaloris, which will be explained in detail in a later chapter. Another reason this program is good for study is because they used the three point lighting plan in all of their shots of Robert Stack and professionally lit the backgrounds behind him so that his face was always the brightest object in the frame. Subtle, but right on target. In a walking shot that is not an easy thing to do.

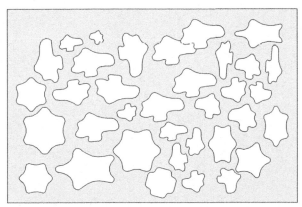

An example of random cut outs of a Cukaloris

Class Exercise

Set up the lighting system that the students will be using and demonstrate how the each part works, the effect of the various functions that the equipment can perform and the proper way to begin the lighting set up and breakdown or 'wrap'.

Each student should then have a hands-on experience with several simple lighting problems and solutions, with the class observing.

Chapter Nine

Sound Recording

The theatre was darker than usual. The scene being played on the screen was a low light, abandoned ship discovered at sea with no crew members. The lead character searched the ship for some sign of life. There was silence with only the occasional creak of the ship and the sound of the actor's footsteps. The actor accidentally touched a radio on a shelf and it came to life with an abnormally loud abrupt sound that made us all jump out of our seats and nervously laugh at our own foolishness, after all it was only a radio. It was only a movie. The film was *The Fog*, by John Carpenter. As a young filmmaker working in films of the same genre, I wondered if the sudden startling sound effect was as powerful as I imagined. The only way to find out was to see the film again at the very next screening. I knew the exact moment when the effect would occur so I waited to study the audience around me to discover why it was so powerful. When it happened I was not able to study the audience as I expected that time either because I jumped again. And I knew it was coming! The jolt was like getting shocked by electricity.

I realized as John Carpenter had already discovered, that you can scare an audience a lot more with sound than you can with images. Especially if they do not expect it is coming. The impact sound has on your audience should not be underestimated.

Three Main Areas of Sound Recording

There are three main areas of sound in any film project, the dialogue or voice over narration, the music score, and the sound effects. The most important of these is of course the dialogue. It is difficult to follow the story without it. The second most important is the sound effects that include the sounds the actors make closing doors, banging dishes, or driving in traffic. Those sounds help the audience feel a part of the action taking place. The third is the music score, which conveys to the audience the emotion of the scene. Omit any one of the three and audience stops 'experiencing' the story.

The Value of Skillful Mixing

It is so annoying to try to hear the dialogue in a feature film when the music score is so loud that you can hardly understand the actors. Or the effects overpower the dialogue in the same way. It is important to keep in mind that the  audience wants to hear the dialogue in order to follow the story, first and foremost, the effects and music can fight for second place as needed by the action on screen. The audience really does not care that you spent a lot of money on the score or that your composer is partially deaf and wants to hear his music louder in the mix. The story is most important and that means the dialogue must be clearly above the other two sound elements. Period. A lot of 'great' filmmakers would disagree with that, but in the end we are the ones buying tickets to see their films, or not.

The Music Score

To be sure, the music score is vital in creating a dynamic addition to your film and until you can afford to hire expensive composers you will have to make due with friends, public domain and 'needle drop' prerecorded music. The best teacher for learning what music to use and how much, is to make a point of concentrating on the music you hear being used in the programs and movies that you watch. By watching a wide variety of types of programs and movies you will begin to sense how professionals use music scores to 'sell' their stories to their audience.

The list for this 'lab' assignment should include a couple of recent blockbuster films, a few old films of the forties and fifties, some episodic TV programs, and if you can find any, some art films from low budget filmmakers of any era. You will learn how to use music and how *not* to use music. My guess is that the forties and fifties movies will fit the latter category. It was a time when composers filled the film with 'wall to wall' musical orchestration with way too many violins and strings of every kind.

Forties and fifties movies-loved the lighting, hated the music!

It is important to note at this point, the value that music performs in your video productions. Without music, your productions seem sparse and incomplete. We have been educated as film goers to presume and expect it as part of the total film experience. Therefore, there are a number of functions it must perform for the audience.

❑ It provides the audience with emotional cues and establishes an atmosphere and mood.

❏ It can provide a continuity and transition from scene to scene, as well as tempo within those scenes.

❏ It can provide the audience with a sense of well being for the character or counterpoint the anxiety of the character.

❏ It can suggest a time in history or a locale of where the scene takes place using our own understanding of people and cultures in our world.

So the choices you make in selecting the type and tempo of the music you want to use in your productions will have far reaching impact on your future audiences. It is a selection that you should make with great care in order to supply the audience with a full and rich experience.

The sound Package

In an age of self contained magic boxes it would seem that considering a sound package as a separate part of the camera package would be unnecessary, however the self contained microphone within the camcorder may not always provide you with the sound that your productions need. For your first productions the camcorder mic may be adequate for recording live sounds and dialogue. No question that these microphones do a good job in capturing the sounds around the camera. Some are so sensitive that they will even record the whirling sound of the zoom motor on the camera or your fingers squeaking the grip on the camera housing. At the family picnic that is not a problem, for your intimate scenes in a quite room it would be distracting to your audience. Most have digital sound capability these days, which creates a wonderfully crisp, (bright) exact, sound, in stereo. For some, that can be almost distracting as well. Train your ear to hear the difference between digital and analogue recorded sound and make your own decision. This is a changing world

constantly in flux so what is true today may not be true tomorrow. For me, and this is just my opinion, the 'warm' sound of analogue recorded dialogue sounds better to my ear than the *too* crisp sound of digitally recorded dialogue. It is a more natural sound, the sound created digitally calls attention to itself. On the other hand, digital sound effects and music sound better to me than analogue recorded sound effects. The effects get muddy in analogue a few generations down, where as analogue dialogue seems to hold up okay.

Most camcorders have an external mic input for hand held microphones, which are usually some variety of a shotgun mic. So named for its shape. In a later chapter we will discuss the technical aspects of microphones in more detail. For now, we will only briefly mention that this type of mic was designed to capture sound in a very narrow direction in front of the mic in order to exclude other sounds, like traffic, not wanting to be recorded along with the actor's dialogue. One way of imagining what the shotgun mic records is to think of the mic as a flashlight on the end of a pole. Everything that narrow beam of light hits will be recorded in sound and that includes what is going on in the distance such as two people talking several feet away. If you can not tell them to shut up, then your sound person wants to turn the mic at an angle so that "beam" misses the two jabber boxes in the distance that do not appreciate the sanctity of filmmaking. On professional shoots the boom operator as they are called, will point the shotgun from above so as to exclude these kinds of extraneous sounds from finding their way to the mic. If there is a shadow problem in having the boom over the actors, then the boom operator will point it up from below which sometimes causes problems from sounds bouncing off the ceiling or even jet planes flying overhead. The bottom line is try to work with your boom operator as much as you can. It is a thankless job and they do the best that they can in providing you with the optimum sound coming into the shotgun mic.

The external mic input can also accept the receiving unit of a wireless mic system in which the actor wears the mic and transmitter. Some inexpensive units do an incredible job for the money, providing you are not in a large city. In which case, you may also receive a trucker's CB or cell phone interference.

For exterior shooting your sound person should never use a shotgun mic without a windscreen. It not only blocks out a lot of the wind noise but also helps block some of the "side" noises coming into the mic. Good earphones are essential in making a professional recording that can be edited. The source of the sound person's earphones should always be down stream from the camcorder so that you know what is actually being recorded not "monitored". A mistake that the sound person can often make if not pre-warned is to have the volume of the headsets turn up high and therefore turn down the recording volume, thus the final playback will be under recorded and create hiss problems in trying to bring the volume up in editing.

All systems should be tested and rehearsed before location shooting. In class at this point would be a good time for all to get hands on experience recording sound and seeing the results on playback. Record sounds the right way and the wrong way as mentioned above to see what problems could be created with just minor changes in volume, placement and various microphones.

Understanding Sound Recording

Most people understand that hard surfaces bounce sound and soft surfaces absorb sound, but few spend any time studying those results in filmmaking. Take a little class time and record sounds in different situations such as carpeted  rooms, hardwood or tiled floored rooms, outside close to a hard wall which will bounce sound and see how it effects your recording. Armed with this experimenting, you will be better prepared for solving location sound problems when they present themselves during your location scouting. Something that I have always done when scouting, is to make a popping sound using my tongue. It is similar to the sound of smacking gum loudly. After I make the sound I listen for the echo made by the loud sound. It tells me what kind of echo problems I will encounter when filming later. Professional filmmakers carry several large sound blankets to spread on the floors and hang around the room when the echo is too noticeable. I once directed an actor while peeping through a sound blanket in a damp basement location because the brick walls were bouncing sound like a reverb unit.

The Value of Hands on Experience

Recording sound, like all the other aspects of filmmaking is by trial and error. A production class is the place to learn this field of study. In a later chapter after you have had some hands on experience we will delve into sound recording and editing in finer detail. After you have had some experiences, you will begin to form the questions that will be answered then. And through that technique of teaching, the answers will stick much better than overloading you right now.

Class Exercise

Set up the sound recording system that the students will be using and demonstrate how the it works, the effect of the various functions that the equipment can perform and the proper way to begin testing the sound pickup.

Each student should then have a hands-on experience with headphones and mic to discover what the sound recording can and can not do, with the class observing.

Chapter Ten

Post Production Considerations

Beginning filmmakers often assume that post production is nothing more than editing your raw footage. For your first project for the most part that may be true. It Is much easier to develop good working habits when the project is simple than when you are under a deadline and waste time in search of an element that has somehow gotten misplaced during the chaotic time you were racing to put your project together.

A Brief History of Film Editing

In a time before you were probably born, we had what were called trim bins that held pieces of 16MM or 35MM film from a few frames long to several yards long. On the same hook or one just above it or some other organizational method we had, were the matching sound cuts for that segment. On other hooks we kept the various takes or insert shots which were assembled by way of a synchronizer and take up reels to create whatever portion of the film we were currently working on at the time. At the same time, a device called a Moviola allowed us to play these segments at sound speed to see the picture and check sync and rhythm.

Once this reel was edited we moved on to the next. The *Star Wars* character name: R2D2 came about because as George Lucas was editing in this style, his reel two picture and dialogue reel two sound were short talked with his assistant editor as R2D2 (Reel 2 dialogue

2). Anyway, unedited film was kept in large film cans in which the roll from the lab was cut into smaller rolls of raw takes, insert shots or sound takes and background sounds on magnetic tape which was carefully labeled with magic marker with the first few lines or key lines of dialogue so we would not have to listen to each roll every time we went to the film can or bin, looking for a particular sound take. In the days when film was physically edited rather than today's method of transferring the raw footage to video and edited it on computers, great organizational care had to be taken to prevent wasting time looking for misplaced footage or mislabeled takes.

In a lot of ways I was fortunate to have had a career that bridged physically editing film to computer aided video editing. Over that span of years there have been many advances to simplify the editing process, reduce the clerical work and provide instant alternate choices. The difficultly of physically editing film in those days had a way of weeding out disorganized and uncommitted wannabe editors. With today's computers anyone can edit so you have a much tougher time competing in  the marketplace because it is so easy to do. The easier a task is, the higher the incompetent will rise in the system before they are discovered. Your best defense against that is to develop skills and practices that place you a cut above the rest. It begins with good work habits, especially in editing.

☐ Prepare the elements in advance of the edit process. These include graphics that may be coming from a different "box".

Camera stand art cards, models, product shots.

Script notes, storyboards, edit lists.

Recorded narration, separately recorded sound effects, music.

Graphics Homework First

It is inefficient and disorganized to begin editing and then stop and go create these missing elements that were, or should have been, listed in your script or on your script notes. Preparing the graphics include the careful check of spelling, punctuation, font type and style and picture composition. All of which can be worked out on a word processor and converted from a printout to the graphics device or software creating the fonts on the screen.

Beginning students often choose font colors based on personal choice rather than what works best for the screen. If the picture has a dark green background behind the area where the graphics should be placed, then dark blue letters, or black will be hard to read on the screen. Putting light blue or white letters against a clouded sky makes equal sense. Think about what your background colors are before choosing your font color. Use a little common sense, you want to use a color that will stand out against the background and that usually means using the opposite color or contrasting color. Another word of caution, red "bleeds" badly on video screens and does not have the crisp edges that lighter colors in the blue and white range have so you should avoid using red except where it is a necessary story point. [Red "Stop!" for example] Mark the script pages to indicate which lines of dialogue are to be wide shot, medium shot and close up (different colored pens help identify each) from viewing the raw footage and studying the script in advance of sitting down in front of the editing computer. This has two advantages. One, you know what you have in the way of choices, and two, you will more likely stick to your preplanned edit list when editing. With today's modern editing computers it is easy to be overwhelmed with choices to the point you forget your original intent. Editing on paper, so to speak, gives you a game plan before starting, which is easy to follow and in most cases, your first thought of how to edit your work is the best one. Along the way you might get a better idea for a shot or a segment and that is to be expected, but at least you will be showing up with direction. Using this technique, you will discover that your work has a better flow and a more professional look than other students that choose the lazy method of just sitting down and "cutting from the hip" so to speak.

Starting the Real Edit

Once all this clerical work is done, you are ready to begin the edit, first make sure your source media is labeled and in the case of still using a cassette tape format that the cassette record tab has been altered so that nothing can be accidentally over recorded. On the "save as" tab in your software program, name your project and save it even before you start and hit the "save" icon often to keep your editing work up to date to insure that if the power goes out you will not lose valuable work. As you make DVD copies of your edited work be proud of your hard work and make it look as professional as you are. The labels on the movies you rent all have professional jackets on them, why shouldn't yours as well? This is the beginning of thinking of yourself as a pro, and it will have a positive impact on you and your work if you do. Think like a pro. Be a pro.

The Edited Master

Once your edited master is ready for screening you want to check it for story problems, dropouts, bad sound segments, misplaced edits, program length and overall impact. One of the most difficult lessons for a beginning editor to learn is: "There is no film(video) that can not be improved with further editing." That usually means cut the length down, not only overall but in individual shots as well. That quote is a double negative. It is so important, let us rephrase it just to be sure you get that. "Every film can be improved with more editing." "But it's perfect, now!" Maybe.

Look at it a few more times and force yourself to fall <u>out</u> of love with that one take you are so crazy about, but deep down know it holds too long. We have all been there at one time or another and it always feels like at the time that you are giving up kinfolk. Be objective, painfully objective. It is the beginning of professional editing.

Advanced Project Assignment

For advanced students, you will want to consider much more about your projects than the basics mentioned above. You will want to consider the emotional impact of your story on the audience and how the audience will feel when the  experience ends with the final credits. These considerations will be covered in detail in a later chapter, for now, an excellent way of working is class critiques to discover if you have met some of you intended goals.

For a lab assignment for advanced students only, write down on a three by five card your basic premise, what emotional intent you had for the audience to grasp and why you feel that was accomplished. After other students have viewed your work they should write down their impressions of the same points mentioned above. Once everyone has had their project screened and gone through the same process, it is time to compare notes. Writing notes on cards keeps everyone 'honest' and free from stating what another classmate has said. It is wise to remember that the others are judging each one of you so stating your opinions fairly and positively will be less painful for all. Try to avoid phrases like: "It was the worst thing I have ever seen!"

This completes the first section of video production. It would be good to review the preceding chapters as you begin your next video project and use the text of these first ten chapters as a guide while you get more hands-on experience in writing, planning, shooting and editing the next project.

Class Exercises

The following is a list of possible real world projects with the kind of experience you can expect in the marketplace. (As a class assignment, all should be under two minutes) The teacher will determine the amount of time to be devoted to these projects.

Lists of Projects

Client One - Wants a short promotional video produced with no dialogue, with background music only, to be played at his or her booth at the next convention for businesses in his or her field.

[Can be a product, service, or franchise]

Client Two - Wants a video to play at the point of sale for some product that will explain a procedure. [Dialogue or graphic explanations]

Client Three - Wants a video to send out to potential customers of one minute in length. [It can be a product, service, or franchise]

Products or services should be ones that you have access to for class.

Part Two

Now that you have completed the first part of this book and discovered the basics of filmmaking, it is time to consider how much you want to be involved in the filmmaking art beyond this course.

For the majority of classes that you are currently taking, it is often difficult to see just how you will be applying what you are learning in the real world after school. The structure of the learning process for those classes makes it even more difficult to visualize their future need.

The entire text for this book has been written, not by an educator, but a seasoned filmmaker with over thirty plus years experience in the business. What you will be learning is not theory as in some courses, but the real applications of these various aspects of the filmmaking process. What you will also learn from these pages is more on the approach of teaching you how to solve and avoid the day to day problems encountered, rather than a step by step, written in stone, set of rules that you experience in Algebra or Physics.

In any endeavor that is so creative, the variables will sometimes override the rules to the point that you will be faced with problems you never would guess could happen. The film, *Wagging the Dog* with Dustin Hoffman is more truth than fiction. To be sure, there are solid answers on how to make movies in this book, but you will also discover that there has been an effort to teach you how to solve filmmaking problems that we would never expect to encounter.

The task is to show you how to solve those problems so that you will not be paralyzed **when**, not if, they occur. You have only to experience an actor dropping dead in the middle of a scene to know just how difficult things can get.

Chapter Eleven

Preparing For Live News Broadcast

In order to adequately prepare for a live news broadcast there are a number of pre-production matters that must be prepared for the program on a regular basis. If it is a complete news broadcast with weather, sports, local news and national or international news segments, each one of those areas must be covered by someone providing the news story, graphics, as well as photos or video segments. For a school situation these may be mock shows in-house or live broadcast going out over a local cable channel, school close circuit, or broadcast via transmission antenna.

Due to the complexity of such an operation, it is necessary to split these various tasks unto several departments. Depending on the size of the class, there may need to be some overlapping of duties based on your local needs.

On-camera anchors may need to be off-camera department heads. For example, it is not uncommon in small local stations to have the sports anchor be responsible for gathering his or her own news material for each broadcast.

The person in command of all of these department heads is the News Producer. (Sometimes called the News Director) Like the editor in chief of a newspaper, this person decides what stories go into the program and allocates the segment running times to each area. On a daily basis, these segments may have a predetermined running time, so news stories have to be timed out to determine if they will fill or run over that time allotment.

In its most simple form, a news program may consist of anchors reading copy with occasional cut aways to a live art stand of still photographs which are loaded before the program and shot as needed by one of the studio camera operators. In its most complicated form, the program will consist of live, on-camera anchors, pre-edited video segments, on screen chroma-keyed weather maps, live remote link-ups, and even commercials or PSAs. The complexity depends on the sophistication of your facility. For this text we will assume the most complex, as it is easy for you to omit the aspects that are not available to you.

Putting on a News Broadcast

Each department has a set of tasks to perform before each program is ready to be aired. The stories to be used on the air, must be researched, written, and supplied with associated graphics and visuals such as file footage for the story, footage shot for the story, or photographs from a file, or photographs shot for this story. As you can see, there are many intricate parts to putting on a news broadcast depending on a number of people doing very specific tasks. In some professional stations involved in this work, the segment directors may also be the on-camera talents, and supervising editors of those segments. Before this complexity gets too far out of hand, we should look at the working chain of command of a typical small news station's department.

- [ ] News Producer-This person brings all of the elements of the program together and decides what will be aired and how much time will be allotted for any given news story, where it will play in the program, and who will announce it on the air. This job is sometimes referred to as the News Director, however that can be confused with the director who directs the actual program airing. For that reason, in this text we will use the term producer.

- [ ] News Director-Controls the production of the program in the booth and follows the script for the broadcast cueing up various videotape recorders or media source computers, art cards, graphics, chroma-keys, and cutaways to other locations.

- [ ] Technical Director-Sits at a console video mixer called a switcher and routes the various video feeds to the program output video/audio signal for broadcast.

- [ ] Studio Camera Operator-One of the studio camera operators concerned with photographing the anchors and live art card easels as needed. The operators generally have headsets that keep them in contact with the booth for instructions from the director.

- [ ] Stage Manager-The stage manager is the eyes, ears and mouth of the director on the floor of the studio. This person wears a headset for instructions from the director and provides silent cues to the on-camera talent for timing instructions.

- [ ] Segment Director-Directs the mini-programs for the news program that are pre-shot, edited, and timed before being cut into the live program.

- **ENG** Camera Operator-Electronic **N**ews **G**athering camera operator. This person generally works in the field with segment directors and on-camera talent.
- Video Editor-This is generally a staff editor who edits several segments for various segment directors.
- Video source Operator-Cues up the various stories or background footage to be played during the broadcast as per the instructions from the technical director and/or the director.
- Graphics Designer-Designs and operates the character generator for live graphics added to the picture going out live on the air.
- Chief Engineer-Is in charge of keeping the technical, electronic equipment working at maximum efficiency for the overall broadcast.
- Any one of these areas may have assistants and/or interns to help in the production of the many parts or as a whole.

Day-to-Day Operations

As you can see there are a number of people required to put even a simple broadcast on the air. Each one has a specific job that all the other members of the team rely on to do their job in a professional way. There is an added pressure of putting on a live program that has a specific time to air regardless of the preparedness of the group. In short, when the big hand on the clock gets to twelve, you're on the air whether you are ready or not. This one aspect of putting on a live program requires so much preparation that it is an important part of the training to put on mock programs for rehearsal for each member. By stepping through each segment with rehearsal, it allows each member to see what the problems are and make corrections without the embarrassment of live screw-ups. (Which are going to happen anyway)

Class Assignment

The first class assignment should be a mock news break-in announcement. The normal procedure is to cut in to a live or taped program with a graphics card and voice over  announcement telling the audience that their regular program is being interrupted for this important announcement. To make your mock breaking news segment more realistic, you may want to have stock footage of a fire, accident, earthquake, robbery in progress, or police chase as your story to report. You need only record a nightly television news program to obtain your mock event.

Even this two-minute to three minute break-in will require several departments to provide assistance. You will need a director, anchor, voiceover announcer, 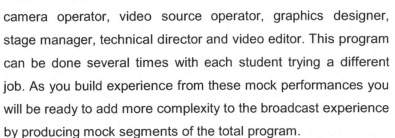 camera operator, video source operator, graphics designer, stage manager, technical director and video editor. This program can be done several times with each student trying a different job. As you build experience from these mock performances you will be ready to add more complexity to the broadcast experience by producing mock segments of the total program.

A good place to start is the opening of the program where all of the anchor talent is on camera for the wide shot opening. Generally speaking, most news broadcast start with national news, so this segment might contain a brief "teaser" as it is called, of the important national news coming up in the next segment after this introduction opening.

Behind the Scenes

A vital part of the efficient running of a live news broadcast is the break time afforded by the commercial breaks. During this time the director will alert the talent about upcoming segments, if the timing is running late certain stories will be dropped, and camera adjustments can be made. For class room situations mock commercials or school PSAs should be incorporated into the show to allow this vital program adjustment time. Since staying on schedule is important for the program to time out with enough material and finish on time, it is important for the producer to be in the booth with a stop watch timing each segment and keeping the director informed of the overall timing. This job should be performed by a senior or experienced student who is a veteran of this classroom-learning situation.

A news anchor can easily adjust their reading speed, and banter with other anchors at the end of a segment to help time out the segment, however, it is wise to have additional copy to cover a discrepancy of thirty seconds or more. One additional story of thirty to forty seconds can fill this need. It would be the last item with a note to read only if prompted to do so to the fill a gap.

Investigative Reporting

The foundation of interesting news programming is the in-depth interview and investigative report. This is all done through segment directors who can have as much time

as necessary to produce a segment for the show unless the topic has some timely interest that must be met immediately.

When the teacher or instructor and the program producer approve a story idea, the segment director will begin research on the topic.

As an example, we will use a story of garbage dumping as a vehicle to show step by step how to produce these kinds of segments.

Your news department hears of a problem a resident in the foothill section of your city has been experiencing with garbage being dumped on the street the night before the usual morning's pick up time. The woman at the address thinks it is vandals, possibly from this school. For that reason, your producer feels that the news department should get to the bottom of the problem to either expose the students involved or vindicate the student body from any wrong doing.

In planning this story, the student producer/segment director (And probably anchor) Visits the homeowner for an interview to hear her side of the story. Next, several neighbors are asked if they have seen anything suspicious on the nights in question. Next, the producer contacts the garbage pickup operator and interviews him for a description of the mess that he refuses to clean up each time it happens. Armed with these interviews, there is but one investigation to do and that is to stake out the location at night to see what in fact is happening. Parked across the street, with camcorder in hand the small crew watches for the criminals to arrive and do their dirty work, harassing this poor elderly lady. As expected, around midnight the vandals arrive, bent on destruction. Two small *raccoons* work together to tip the can over and rummage through the garbage looking for food.

What started out as an investigative report has turned into a human-interest story. Ending with wonderful shots of the raccoons at work-or is it play?

This is the kind of story that could make national news if handled correctly. Let us break it down the way a professional would investigate this story.

First, you have serious interviews with several parties that can be edited in a number of ways. Since this has a somewhat comedic outcome, you want to keep in mind that comedy is a series of set ups and payoffs. If you are not familiar with this term, it means that a joke is 'set up' (the back story) and then paid off with the punch line. Your set up in this case is the serious interviews with residents. The payoff is the discovery that it is raccoons, not vandals. You want to be careful not to hold the public up to ridicule by showing them as accusatory of some group and then showing them as fools when it turns out to be harmless. This is what would happen it you edit in only inflammatory kinds of comments by the parties involved. Care should always be taken in taste and fairness to the public. Integrity and trust is the cornerstone of news reporting.

Regardless of the cute outcome, it is a serious problem for the elderly lady who may not be in good enough health to be picking up garbage, so a kind word about how to protect your trash cans from these kinds of bandits would be a good way to end the story along with a thank you to the parties involved.

Most investigative reports do not have a amusing outcome but the above recommendations still apply.

Editing the Investigative Report

In editing this kind of reporting, you want to study the interviews to gleam what is the essence of the interview that clearly states what the interviewee is expressing. Once these  important facts have been isolated, you then can build a narrative of what the story is about. An old adage in newspaper reporting is: Who? What? When? Where? and How? If you remember to cover these questions in your report, you will find it easier to get to the bottom of your story.

So the basics of field reporting are:

☐ Interview as many related parties as possible. Eye witnesses, victim, victim's neighbors. Opposing parties if there is a dispute.

☐ Make your own independent investigation whenever possible. Find out the facts on your own.

☐ Study the raw footage from the interviews to find what is essential to be reported in the shortest number of words possible. A detail of the color of dress the person was wearing is not necessary. As Sgt. Friday frequently said on Dragnet: "Just the facts, ma'am."

☐ Approach the editing of the piece as an objective bystander looking only for the truth or what is fair to all parties. No matter what view you take if you do not take this approach will result in negative response from the public. Half the time, it will anyway.

Once it has been edited to time, take a second look with these things in mind:

☐ One, is it clear to the public that knows only the information you give them? Two, can it be shorten any more because more than likely it is too long. Look again.

☐ As cute as it is, avoid putting too much music underscored. Less is more.

☐ Remember: Every story has a beginning, middle and end. Have you told the story in a clear, simple way that will not be confusing to your audience? Save your convoluting, highly detailed documentary skills for when you are out on your own. This is a newscast and every second is precious.

Class Exercise

Just as these rules apply to the field segment, from a storytelling point of view, the news stories being read on the air should go by the same rules.

Once these basic skills have been practiced a few times, it is time to try a dress rehearsal of a complete broadcast, to be taped and critiqued by the whole class. With this experience, the next step is to pre-record a newscast to be aired. With this success, the next step is to venture into your first live broadcast. By this time, everyone should have enough experience to be more at ease with a live broadcast.

Chapter Twelve

More Advanced Script Writing

In chapter one you learned that scripts can be broken down into simple sections called the beginning, middle and end. That was made overly simple in order to supply your needs then. Now we will expand that concept into its proper form called the three-act play. Most often in films you see, this transition from act to act is seamless so you do not see it as three separate acts. Sometimes it is punctuated by a fade to black or a dissolve from one section to the next. Generally, there is a passage of time, although that is not mandatory.

The Three-Act Screenplay

In act one, the premise is presented and the main or key characters are established. We meet the protagonist and the antagonist. The problem is presented. Which is what we call the *plot*.

Premise Example: We are in a raft heading down a river.

In act one, at the beginning, it is mandatory that we meet the antagonist so that we, as the audience, do not feel that bad writing is cheating us if he were to pop in at the last minute in act three. What I call *situational* writing. Situational writing is a string of unrelated events (scenes) that do  not move the story to a climatic end. It is one pitfall that beginning writers often fall into in their attempt to create a story. A popular film to use as an example of very good writing is *The*

Bone Collector, starring Denzel Washington as a completely paralyzed, bed-ridden detective. When did we <u>first</u> see the antagonist in *The Bone Collector? At the end of the first scene sequence.*

So even though we do not find out it is he until the end of act three we have met him in the first act. He was the character who came in to repair and monitor the sophisticated medical equipment keeping Mr. Washington's character alive. If the antagonist had simply killed our lead character at the beginning when he had a perfect opportunity, we would not have had much of a story. And as we stated before, each <u>act</u> has a beginning, middle and end, which we should use to build to a climax for each act.

In act two the problem intensifies. At the beginning of act two we present the audience with what is often called the *Or Else Factor.* If we do not solve the problem something bad will happen-perhaps the raft will sink and we all die. The *or else factor* is the formula that drives <u>all</u> the movies that you have seen.

Or Else Factor Example: We see rapids ahead as we head down the river. We lose an oar. Water gets into the raft. A secondary character has a heart attack.

In *Atomic Train* a runaway train is headed for Denver with an atom bomb on board, if they cannot stop the train before Denver, millions will die. A classic *or else factor.* Just presenting the *or else factor* is not enough to sustain the storyline so you must invent ways to turn up the heat for the protagonist as act two unfolds. If you think about movies or TV shows that you did not like, if you go back and reexamine their story structure you will more than likely see that they failed to turn up the heat on the central characters in act two. The key element for act two is intensify, intensify, intensify. Remember: *Without conflict **there is no** drama.* Conflict is the key element in developing your story, without it, the story will begin to fall flat and your audience will lose interest. Each scene can have its own conflict and resolve. Constantly building as your story unfolds.

Very often within act two you will see a particular scene, which is mandatory, if you expect to sell your story both to your audience and the powers that be. It is called the confrontation scene and every good story has one. This is a scene between the protagonist and the antagonist where they, in effect, draw the line in the sand and clarify the importance of the *or else factor* and how it is vitally important to each. Often the antagonist will make some declaration like "tomorrow you die" or in a classic teen movie- "I'm beating you up after school". They part their ways and the protagonist prepares for the big day. The audience vicariously frets along with the protagonist about how they are going to get out of that mess.

Are you surprised that you were being fed the same formula in every movie?

An utterly far-fetched confrontation scene that the audience buys completely is the one in *Heat* starring Al Pacino and Robert De Niro. Pacino is a cop and De Niro is a bank robber. They meet in a coffee shop toward the end of act two and draw the line in the sand where both declare that each respects the other but neither will hesitate to blow the other one away if they meet during a robbery.

Utterly far-fetched for the simple reason, cops do not meet with criminals that way, not even high profile ones like that, but who cares, this is De Niro and Pacino in confrontation at their best, and this **is** drama. If you are paying close attention and realize that you are watching **the** confrontation scene, you can easily see what the writer is telescoping (as it is called) to you about how it is all going to turn out. *Heat* was written and directed by Michael Mann. Excellent.

In act three we have what is called *resolving the conflict*. This is the high intensity, dramatic finale to our story where several important things must happen. It should be noted that each act should build more than the previous act, the tempo of the pace should be increased. Even though act two is often the longest act.

Several important things must happen in act three. The story builds to a climax, the situation is resolved for good or bad, and the protagonist must confront the antagonist alone. And most importantly, the protagonist must be the one to beat the antagonist. It must be the protagonist who kills, takes to justice, or exposes the antagonist. *Why*?

The audience has become the protagonist as they follow the story and they feel cheated if they are not vindicated or allowed to win through the acts of the protagonist. It is the least you can do since you have made them suffer along with the central character. When the protagonist is "saved" by someone else or by some outside force, the audience finds themselves saying: "Where did that come from?" Rather than having the satisfaction of the feeling that they (through the character on screen) have saved mankind or whatever your *or else factor* happens to be.

Now if the formula is so simple and we have certain rules that must be followed, why do we keep making movies and why do we keep going to see them?

The answer is: The writer has at his or her disposal all the layers that make up human nature, circumstances or situations, and opportunity. We can make each story as complex as we think the audience can follow, we can use a variety of time periods, we can place our protagonists in a variety of social, professional and political situations, and we can tell our story in a variety of linear ways. Chronologically, as a flashback, juxtaposition or a combination of the three.

We can have an 'A' story and a 'B' story. Epics sometimes have a 'C', 'D', 'E' stories (*Independence Day*) and so on. So it is through all of these elements that we add texture, fascination, and distinctiveness to <u>our</u> story. You are familiar with the term *cause and effect*. The character is the *cause* and the plot is the *effect*. Remember that in good writing, the characters control the plot, not the other way around.

We really could spend a whole semester on this subject and deal with much more than what we are just barely scratching the surface with in this chapter. I would encourage you to find more about it on your own. The best book ever written on the subject of screen writing is *Writing the Script* by Wells Root. Find it.

Apply it to what you will be learning in other literary studies. You will be delighted to see that these elements have been with us for a long time for a very good reason. **They work.** And it will help you understand your material on a much deeper level as you begin to see that whether it is a script, a novel or dramatic play it all comes back to the character and plot which creates the storyline. As Shakespeare put it so well: "The play is the thing in which I will catch the consciousness of the King."

The play is the thing!

Now, we are going to get into the specifics of your scripts and how to create your next video. Before we do that let us review the basics of script writing from chapter one.

Act one

The Premise should:

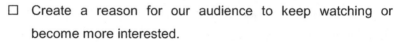

- ☐ Establish the kind of story we are about to tell.
- ☐ Establish the characters we want our audience to know.
- ☐ Present the audience with our premise.
- ☐ Create a reason for our audience to keep watching or become more interested.

For the type of programs you are about to create, the first act premise should serve the purpose of presenting your problem to the audience. It should be one clear direct sentence. This applies to dramatic plays, documentaries, commercials, public service announcements, and short subject presentations.

Act Two

Act two of our script should ask the audience some questions and present ways of solving the problem we have presented in the beginning. The second act is the main body of the program. If you allow yourself to indulge too long with the  presenting of the problem, you run the risk of losing your audience altogether. In their mind they begin to say: "This is too overwhelming." and tune out. It is important to see the progress of the story and know when you have spent too much time on the problem without offering any help, or shown too many examples of the problem without offering any possible solutions. The audience begins to say to themselves: "Okay, I get your point, let's move on, for Pete's sake!"

Act two of our story fulfills these important needs:

- ☐ We intensify the problem through examples.
- ☐ We allow our audience to ask questions mentally from the material we have presented.
- ☐ We give them some glimmer of hope that this situation can be resolved in a positive way.

Act Three

Act three of your story is the wrap up. You have presented your problem, you have shown examples of the problem and now you need to present solutions, hope and some kind of  resolve for good or bad in the case of a dramatic story. For commercials and public service announcements (PSA), we have what is called in the advertising business, as *the call to action*. You have been subjected to the 'call to action' most of your lives while watching commercials. The typical: "If you call in the next fifteen minutes, we will send you *two* of these really crumby things that won't actually work." Or: "Don't miss out on this great offer, come by today..."

Act three should provide these needs:

- ☐ The finale to the problems we have been intensifying in act two.

☐ The resolve of the problem for good or bad of the central character.

Recapping what we have just covered, consider the following aspects of the writing process:

☐ What is the purpose of the script?

☐ What are the various elements of the script?

☐ What is the importance of the wrap up?

☐ What is the call to action?

The Importance of an Outline

One of the best ways to start a script is to begin with an outline. The outline should be a simple road map of where you want to go in your presentation. To start that process ask yourself the following questions:

☐ What is the purpose of the production?

☐ What are the basic elements of the production?

☐ Does the story lead to a climax, and some resolve? [In the case of a dramatic story]

☐ Does the production lead to a call to action? [In the case of a commercial or PSA]

Once these basic elements are solidified in your mind the story will begin to take shape. With practice, this process will become much more easy in time.

This review from chapter one should take on a new meaning now that you have a better understanding of the process of screen writing with its complexities and layers for you to create, for your audiences to unravel with interest and concentration.

Class assignment: Create a two-minute movie about a character you have met.

Chapter Thirteen

Pre-production Details

Just as your perception of screenwriting has become more acute, so the level of understanding of all the other aspects of filmmaking will develop. When you have completed a script that you will be producing you will need to break the script elements down into all the basic requirements of the script which includes the number of actors, locations, props, vehicles, animals, and special wardrobe to name a few.

Numbered Shot Shooting Script

The illustration shows a typical script page, noting location, time of day, scene description, actors involved, dialogue, and shot number located on the far right side of the location description. On a number of actual script pages used in the industry, the shot numbers will appear on both sides of the page. Although studios may have a good reason for that extra number on the left side of the page, it is more efficient, and simpler for you to use just the one on the right side. The importance of using a numbered shot script is in order to list each scene in the shooting schedule. Often in scripts there is a reoccurrence of a location and scene. The numbered script lets you know which scene you are shooting at any one time. It also makes it easier to plan the shooting sequence when the same location is used more than once. Since lighting, actors, props and furniture may all be involved in shooting a particular location, it is much easier to film them all at the same time rather than returning to the same location over and over during the entire filming process. This is one reason films are shot completely out of sequence. Often it is the availability of the star that determines the shooting order, but it also is determined by the location and set requirements. The amount of time required to set up the camera and lighting for a location is such that it is frequently more time efficient to have the actor change their wardrobe for a new scene (and maybe a new day) at that location than to come back later and reset lighting, power requirements and camera equipment.

FADE IN

EXT. STREET CORNER-ESTABLISHING SHOT-DAY   26

    The "Don't Walk" sign is blinking. A student wearing a backpack looks at his watch
nervously, and then back at the blinking sign. He looks around as he steps closer to the curb.

EXT. OPOSITE STREET CORNER   - DAY   27
    WIDE ON a cop in a squad car across the street, watches the youth as he approaches the curb.

EXT. STREET CORNER - Continuous   28
    On the student as he places one foot out into the street and looks for cars when he notices the cop eyeing him.

ANGLE   27A
    Close on the cop's face as he shakes his head no at the student.

ANGLE   27A
    CLOSER ON the student as he sheepishly pulls his foot back and plants it on the curb.

EXT. STREET CORNER - Continuous   29
    On a two shot of another pedestrian standing close to the student having witnessed the visual encounter.

PEDESTRIAN
Cops! They're always around when you don't want one.

CUT TO:

Script Breakdown

The first order of business after completing the script is to analyze it in regards to getting the project on film or DVD or even videotape. This is called breaking the script down. One of the best Production Designers in the business, William Strom, with whom I have had the pleasure of working on several projects over the years, does the most methodical job of dissecting a script I have ever seen. On my scripts, he would ask detail questions about the actor's wardrobe, props that were only vaguely mentioned in the script, locations descriptions and camera angles, what was expected to be seen in the background or not seen, and more and more details. When he finished asking me all of his various questions, I felt I had been through a tax audit. They were all important questions that the art department needs to know in order for the shoot to be prepared long before the crew and actors arrive. His approach is to read between the lines and get the subtext of the story. That is, for example, the script calls for a car. What kind of car? What is the income level of the character, is it a sports car, a station wagon, a piece of junk?

So breaking down the script is much more than just listing the items that are easy to spot scanning the script pages. It is looking for what has been omitted in telling your story on the printed page and bringing it to life visually. As a director of your project, this kind of careful scrutiny will aid you in developing the layers and textures of your screenplay. It will help you visualize just how you want your actors to dress, the locations to look, the mood of the lighting to use, and even the color ranges for a total visual impact. If you saw *Dick Tracey* you will remember that the art department used only primary and secondary colors for all the colors seen on screen to heighten the comic book look of the film. As a student filmmaker you may not care or have the time to take for this kind of detail. If you begin to dissect your scripts in this manner, you will find later on that your projects have a more professional look than other student's projects because you are seeing more layers and textures. More ways of expressing your cinematic thoughts for your audiences. Who can question the brilliant visual details of *Blade Runner*, directed by Ridley Scott. I know from talking with people that worked on the picture that he personally was responsible for the complete visual look of the film. His background was Art Directing, which is a visually demanding endeavor, so that is not much of a surprise. *Blade Runner* has layer after layer of visual details, from wardrobe to vehicles, from background signs to search lights, Scott saw it all and put it all on film using his talented crew of craftspeople to carry out his remarkable vision. All of this comes from breaking down the script and seeing not just what is there, but what is *not* there.

Shooting Schedule

The shooting schedule for any motion picture is based on resolving all of the production shooting problems presented by the availability of the actors, the locations, timeline problems (Changing an actor's look over the period of the film, for example), the most efficient use of shooting the scenes in a certain order, and sometimes the availability of certain crewmembers. There can even be delays due to the availability of certain props or vehicles. The key people involved in these decisions are the unit manager (UM) and the first assistant director(1st. A.D.) with input from the director and producer for special problems. There are specially designed production boards with movable strips that have the scene numbers, actors, locations and number of script pages listed on each strip. These are stacked in a row so that the continuity of actors, locations, props, extras and so on can be viewed at a glance and moved about as needed. There are no doubt computer programs in laptops on locations right now providing the same information as well. These programs are designed for a rather small segment of our society so they will no doubt be expensive. For your needs, any plan that allows you to see several scenes at once will be of help to you. The important factor is to be able at a glance to see where there is an overlap of actors, locations, extras or special needs that will help you make a decision on what to shoot first and in what order is most efficient use of time and resources.

Art Department Notes

On most of your first projects you may be the director, cinematographer, and art department all rolled into one. All the more reasons to take careful notes before planning your shooting. Before the pressure of the shoot comes is the time to have those brilliant ideas. With the right amount of lead-time, you may actually have time to prepare the art department's needs in order to get them on film or video media. The art department provides the visual input to help you tell your story in so many nonverbal ways. A number of art directors, production designers, and visual consultants have gone on to be exceptional film directors. The Scott brothers, Tony and Ridley to name just two.

Pre-production Meetings

Last minute planning results in sloppy, disorganized filmmaking in which all of your lack of planning shows up on the screen for all to see. It will be visually uninteresting, poorly told, amateurishly directed, and therefore badly acted, and generally unprofessional. Alfred Hitchcock once said that when he finished his "book" the movie was over for him. The *book* was his notebook in which his storyboard artists had drawn from his instructions all of his shots, showing how the camera was to move, what kind of transition would be made from scene to scene, what would or would not be seen in the frame, what lens would be used, how the actors would look and what they would wear, what the location would be and what matt shots would block any background visual information he did not want in the frame, any rear screen projections to be used, and so on. No wonder he felt the project was over for him, he only had to look at his notebook to see the movie in its entirety. Few directors are that prepared.

Preparing for Pre-production Meetings

There are a number of things you need to prepare before your production meeting with the rest of your crew as stated above. It begins with having a clear understanding of your script and the story you want to tell. If you do not have a clear vision of how the story should be told, how do you expect the crew to know what is expected of them? If you are not excited and believe in the project, why should your crew? If you are not forceful enough to be a leader, how do you expect the crew to follow? Directing is not for everyone, but it is important for everyone at your level of filmmaking to give it an honest try. The last thing you want to do is wake up twenty years from now and say: "Why didn't I at least try?"

If you have a vision and a passion for filmmaking, let that drive you rather than letting your shyness or lack of self confidence hold you back. All the other "stuff" will fall into place.

As you prepare for your production meeting, arm yourself with the knowledge of your story that the others do not know. Do this by studying the script, visualizing the way you want to shoot it, see in your mind's eye how the frame should look, and how you want to tell your story. These are the things your crew will want to know at that meeting. The following is a list of what you should expect to accomplish at your first pre-production meeting:

☐ Have the cast read the script through for the director and crewmembers.

☐ After the script has been read, ask for questions.

☐ Have the director explain any special needs from the cast or crew.

☐ Agree upon all of the decisions made from the above material.

☐ Decide on the availability of all the cast and crewmembers for the shooting schedule.

☐ Lock down all the variables of locations, actor and crew availability, and art department needs.

In Detail

"Have the cast read the script through for the director and crew members." - In some cases, this will be the first time the actors and crew members will be meeting each other and the script. This will give the director a feel for hearing the written words as

others say them.

"After the script has been read, ask for questions." - The script should raise questions from the cast members and the department heads. "What do you mean by this?" "How do you want to show that?" "Where do we get one of those?" Questions better raised at this meeting than when the crew is waiting to shoot.

"Have the director explain any special needs from the cast or crew." - It is difficult to put everything in the writer's mind on paper so it is important for the director to explain his or her vision for this story. That may include special effects, special props, special points of views of the camera, or generally anything that is not clear on the printed page.

"Agree upon all of the decisions made from the above material." - Your crew is a vital part of seeing your project come into being so make sure you have their support and understanding. Everyone involved wants to see the project succeed so value his or her input. Listen to what they have to say. They just may have a better way of giving you exactly what you want.

"Decide on the availability of all the cast and crew members for the shooting schedule." - Everyone's schedule will be different and difficult to coordinate in order to get your project made. One tip from an old timer: The more time you lose, the more momentum you lose until finally the project never gets finished. Keep it moving from the beginning and do not slow down until it is done, otherwise you will wake up to the realization that it probably never will get done. There will be one problem after another.

"Lock down all the variables of locations, actor and crew availability, and art department needs." - Just as the above, lock

it down and get it moving before one delay causes another delay.

Call Sheets for Actors and Crew Members

Once the outcome of your pre-production meeting has determined all of the above, it is time to create your call sheets for your actors and crewmembers. Again, on your first projects this may seem like over kill, especially if there is only one actor. Never the less, make it a habit to go through the motions so that as your projects become more complex you will already be used to handling your shoots professionally. When you work on real feature films you will come to expect the vital information contained in the call sheet. [See Illustration in Appendix A]

The call sheet should contain the call time (The time that a given person is expected to arrive at the location or set.) for the various crewmembers, the actors, special equipment or vehicles and the shooting order of the scenes. These times may vary greatly for each member of your team. Common sense should alert you to the fact that makeup, hair and wardrobe should get there and be set up before the actors arrive. The camera and lighting crew should get there and be set up before the actors walk onto the set and expect to begin filming. You certainly do not want the police car and officer to get there and wait for hours until all these other things have happened. Your shoot should be planned around you most expensive asset, and everything else built around that asset. If you have access to a squad car (Local police or campus) or some other public aid, you want them to be inconvenienced as little as possible. That means planning your time and shooting schedule so that you are set up and waiting when they arrive, shoot their angles first, and get them wrapped up first. In the future it will be much easier to ask for their help again for other student projects.

"Don't poison the well you are drinking from." As the saying goes.

Class Assignment

Make up a call sheet for a one day shoot on location at the city hall of your city for a crew including the D.P. with two assistants, Gaffer and best boy, sound and boom operator, three person art department, Make up and hair dresser, one wardrobe person, two star actors, three secondary actors, twelve extras, a director, producer, script supervisor, prop master and one assistant, cater and three interns. Figure out how many people that requires for lunch.

Camera and lighting set up require one hour, actors need to be on set ready to shoot at 8:30, having been through make up, hair and wardrobe. (Decide how much time should be allotted for each.) Back time the calls for the crew so that you know when the call time for the crew should be. Art department needs to be at location one half hour before lighting and camera crew.

Parking for the location is across the street. Crew should be alerted to keep their parking stub for reimbursement. They will need the address.

Pre-production Budget

For student projects, the extent of the pre-production budget may be so limited that it would be of no use as a teaching tool. It should be mentioned as a vital part of the process. Columbia College in Los Angeles teaches a course in budgeting film productions. It was difficult to cover all that was needed in one quarter. (They are not on the semester system) There are budgeting books that will give you the vital information you need if you plan a feature film that will include Screen Actor's Guild (SAG) contract agreement payments, daily scale for crew members, film stock, liability insurance, post production cost, editing cost, music rights and contracts, catering, dressing room and honey wagon expenses, and teamsters costs to name a few. As you can see with this brief list, there is too much to cover in this text on pre-production cost estimating.

Script Rehearsal

Acting on film is much more difficult than stage acting due to the splicing up of the actor's performance into tiny segments to put on film. For that reason, your actors need rehearsal time with the director. Understanding how to play the part on film is not an experience your actors should have to have while the crew is standing around waiting. The rehearsal with the director should occur long before the time to shoot has come. You will be directing for the first time in most cases and you will be directing students that have little if any experience acting on film. They may have had some experience acting in class plays and therefore have more experience than you, however you have a vision for how you want to tell your story, which they do not have. What all of this boils down to is this, you must learn to trust each other, help each other, work with each other, if you want the project to succeed. I have heard many directors claim that they are against "over" rehearsing actors or that they like to come to the set unprepared so it will be more "spontaneous". Amazingly, none of these "shoot from the hip" types ever win Oscars. Why is that?

Class Assignment

Blocking a scene for camera.

Break up into a few small groups to form a few 'production companies'. If there are actors in the class who would like to volunteer to be directed by a student director, then proceed that way. If not, then have two students be actors without lines in a situation listed below. The scene should be not longer than one minute with camera and actor movement.

Try these Situations:

1) Two students walk into a restaurant hang out. One goes to a counter to order food. The other walks over to a jukebox to play a song, then joins his or her friend at the counter. Your job is to make that as interesting as possible. It can be with or without dialogue depending on your volunteers.

2) Two students walk into a bank. One goes to a teller window to cash a check. The other walks over to the table with deposit slips and pens, then discovers that they have lost their check. Make this interesting without dialogue.

3) Two students walk into a doctor's office, one goes to the receptionist's window where they are given a clipboard with a form to fill out. The other one sits down in a chair and picks up a magazine. When the friend joins the waiting student, they discuss the form to the annoyance of other patients. Make this interesting without planned dialogue. Ad-lib what is funny on the form.

Chapter Fourteen

Scouting for Locations

The term "location" generally refers to a distant place where the film company photographs a locale for its look that matches the requirements of the script. For student productions that might simply mean anywhere that is off campus. When motion picture companies move to a distant location that is out of state they will often try to use the locale for all of their filming requirements. For example, should they need the Grand Canyon as a backdrop for a major part of their story, then they may very well seek out a warehouse in a nearby town to use as a sound stage for other parts of the story. If not, then perhaps an office building, or a grocery store, a mall, or some other locale that fits the script. There are a number of reasons for doing this besides the efficiency of shooting related scenes together. "Hollywood" is a street wise town, meaning if you want to shoot anywhere in Los Angeles, you will pay heavy for the location, you will be required to pay off-duty police officers for traffic control, you will need city permits, you may need to pay an off-duty fire marshal to insure that your electric cables for lighting are safe, and so on. For that reason, more and more film companies are moving out of town to shoot. In smaller towns across the country, the people are glad to have the film money come to town, the police will often help you for free and the location fees are less expensive if at all. For the individuals involved in the location scouting, there are a number of requirements that must be on their minds as they look at any one location, such as power for lights, a place to park company trucks, sound problems, background vistas, availability for the duration of filming, and accessibility for all the camera angles that might be required.

While location scouting with a film crew in the everglades in Florida one summer, we pulled up to a small deserted cabin that looked like it fit our script perfectly. So perfect, the art department would have to do very little to dress the set. We sat in the van talking about all the advantages of this location, until someone suggested we take a closer look. As we approached the cabin we began to see hundreds, if not thousands of mosquitoes landing on us. We all turned in unison to the van and someone glibly remarked that this location would not work after all.

Scouting locations well in advance has its merits and its pitfalls. Things can change from scout to shoot. William Strom, an exceptional Production Designer was working on *A Killer in the Family*, starring Robert Mitchum and James Spader. The script called for a rundown mobile home in disrepair. Strom found the perfect location, complete with torn curtains on the windows and rusted metal siding. The location manager made the deal with the owner and Strom told them just how perfect the location would be for what they wanted. He even made a point to tell them not to touch a thing. A couple of weeks later they were ready to shoot the mobile home. Strom arrived early to add finishing touches and dress the location. To his horror, the owner had painted the exterior, hung new curtains, cleaned up the yard, and generally destroyed what they had envisioned for the look of that location. He had no choice but to trick up the location as fast as possible. He was lucky to find the torn curtains in the trash, and spread other trash on the yard and used water-based paint to make the newly painted metal siding look rusted and weathered again. It was a no win situation in which he did the best he could. When the director arrived he remarked that Strom could have found a better location, he thought Strom understood he wanted something that looked more rundown.

When you look for your locations you will be on a no budget situation so your location possibilities will be much more limited. If you need a drugstore aisle for your script, as a student filmmaker you will find that you, as the camera operator, and your actor(s) may be able to just walk in and shoot your scene as though you are just clowning around with a camera, providing you do not bring in a crew and try to act like a Hollywood film company. As a student, most employees will not mind, providing you do not destroy property in the process. Keep in mind that other people in the store do not care to be reluctant extras so keep them out of frame and respect their privacy. I will not advise you on whether or not you should ask the store manager in advance for permission to shoot. Shooting incognito sort of falls into the *don't ask, don't tell* category. If your camcorder looks like a consumer camcorder you will likely be able to get by with less hassle. In any case, do not leave the store without buying *something*.

Other locations may have insurance liabilities or trespassing on private property issues that will preclude your use of such areas without proper permission. Public areas such as parks are a good place to use, keeping in mind that others deserve their privacy. Shooting in the park and videotaping a man kissing his coworker in the background could cause you more problems than you want.

Breaking the law for any reason in order to facilitate your story is unacceptable, unprofessional and extremely unwise. You may find at some time in the future that you need the police to help you in a shoot. It will be difficult to get their cooperation then if they already know you as a troublemaker, so do not burn those bridges by doing something stupid as a beginner.

Location Potentials

Before beginning any location scouting you should write down exactly what you want. Having a clear picture in your mind's eye will help you spot what you need when you see it. The potential location should have several camera angle possibilities in case you encounter problems when you get there to shoot. Getting set up with camera gear, actors and crew is a lot of work so it is always wise to look for locations that fit more than one need. That can include altering the script's setting to allow you to use something else nearby. Be open to ideas that will allow you to shoot several scenes at one location. For example: Let's say you have one scene that calls for a parking lot location downtown and you have another scene that calls for a fast food restaurant location in the suburbs. Across from the downtown parking lot stands an old restaurant with a lot more character. As long as you have to drive downtown and set up, maybe the restaurant across the street would be more interesting anyway. Always be on the lookout for ways of improving your film visually and decreasing your workload from unnecessary location hopping.

Years ago I needed a cemetery location for a scene for my feature, upon checking with the owner of one, I was informed that there was no cemetery in Los Angeles that would allow another crew to shoot. When I asked why, I was informed that a major studio had recently shot in one. After they wrapped, the owner discovered headstones turned over, soda and beer cans left all around and generally left a mess for the cemetery owner to clean up. The cemetery association put the word out to ban film crews from location shooting. Clean up the mess you make at a location and make sure you leave it in better shape than you found it, if you expect to use locations in the future.

Some Practical Advise

The saying goes: "Give a man a fish, you feed him for a day. Teach a man to fish, you feed him for a lifetime." Illustrations are one of the best ways to teach and as stated in the introduction to this section of the book there are so many variables in  the creative art of filmmaking the only real way to prepare you for those problems out there is to teach you to think on your feet.

Using the example of the downtown location scout above, let us consider that whole scenario. Let's say your scene calls for a young man working at the fast food hamburger joint who has a girl friend come to visit him at work. The scene calls for him to be discovered by her in the back of the restaurant cleaning out the mop bucket. She arrives and they sit down and talk. He's frustrated that his life is going nowhere, he fears that he's going to spend the rest of his life cleaning mop buckets. She tries to be supportive.

Not too exciting a scene and we make only one point, he does not want to spend his life doing this. On top of this choice of locations we have the added problem of sound recording only a few feet from the drive-thru order panel that

is always at the rear of those places. The constant squawk from the order speaker can make sound recording impossible.

Now consider that other location downtown, a seedy little dive of a restaurant with an alley next to the back door. Our character cleans the mop in the dark, smelly, alley. Our visuals are getting more interesting. We see the girl friend approach the foreboding alley with concern. Will she be mugged on the way to her boy friend? He is embarrassed for her to find him there. They sit on a trashcan and he says that he does not want to spend his life in this alley. We cut to another angle where we see a bum hiding in a pile of trash that is hearing those words. He takes a drink from his bottle and thinks about the possibility of spending the rest of his life in this alley. He pours the drink out. We have added several more layers to our story because we have shown the real fears of our young mop jockey, how his life could really end up. We have shown that the drunk maybe sees himself as this young man and wonders how it all went wrong. We show that maybe the young man's determination has encouraged the bum to straighten out his life and gives him new hope.

By just changing your location you have told your story in a more compelling way, you have brought in more layers and textures, you have made it more visually interesting, and in all likelihood found a quieter place to shoot.

Turning Compromises into Improvements

The point of the preceding illustration is to encourage you to use the compromises you will have to make in scouting locations to improve your project with better visuals and more dynamic storytelling. Look for ways to make it more interesting with the world around you, whether that is a small town or a big city.

Sometimes sitting in front of your iPod or word processor as you write your story, it is difficult to visualize the best location. That is to be expected. As you scout for locations, be open to those sudden inspirations that will bring your story to life. For that reason, your first location scout should be alone so that you can think about the possibilities available to you. Filmmaking is a creative art and location scouting is one that is best done, first alone, and then amplified by the support of the others you want involved in the project. Bouncing ideas off of each other leads to more creativity and soon the film becomes exciting beyond the original concept you struggled to create at the word processor. That is what makes filmmaking thrilling, creative, and worthwhile.

Class Assignment

Create a list of possible local locations for a film company to shoot for a script requirement. Shoot stills or raw video footage of the location with a one-page report on the advantages of using this location for the film company. The  report should include possible alternate shooting advantages this location affords the company.

Chapter Fifteen

Preparing the Location for Filming

There are few locations where you can just arrive and start shooting. Almost all require some preparation. It could be as simple as a park location that requires moving a picnic table for a better angle or out of the sun into the shade. If your project includes an art department, they want to arrive at the location early enough to be able to  prepare the location for filming. A lot of that kind of work is a thankless job so the last thing that they need is double work because you were not well prepared as the director. If you do not have an art department on your shoot, you may be it. It is important that all concerned should know the shooting order of the sequences being photographed to avoid that double work of moving things first one way and then the other. The call sheet has that information on it and should be adhered to as much as possible.

If the scene calls for a car in a certain position, or some set piece to be placed a certain way, then you want to make sure it works for the D.P. and the director long  before the day of the shoot. That will allow the art department to have it set up and ready to light when the crew gets there. Most art directors and set decorators like to work in layers as they prepare a location for shooting. First the key elements are placed as agreed to in pre-production meetings and location scouts. Then they will fine-tune the elements. In the case of a picnic table it would mean placing the tablecloth and props. For a cardboard box from which a bum emerges, it might mean trash bags and papers placed around the box. Graffiti covered over on the brick wall behind the box. From  broad strokes to finer details until the level of realism they are seeking is reached. This usually occurs as the lighting crew and camera people are setting up the camera and related equipment. After the director has had a run through with the actors and the lighting crew are fine tuning their set up, the set decorator will make final adjustments for the scene. On professional film crews this will occur with a minimum of talking. As a matter of fact you can usually judge the professionalism of the company by the lack of talking. This is out of respect for the director and actors who are also fine tuning their performance with last minute rehearsals. The sound recorder and boom operator are working out their moves and problems as well, so the quieter the crew, the better they can rehearse following the actor's sounds. As student filmmakers you want to learn to work quietly and efficiently as you do your particular job. This will keep you from embarrassing yourself when you work on a feature film crew.

Preparing the Set for Filming

Unless your school has a sound stage, your first experiences shooting on sets will be your family's house, a friend's business, or some other

location interior that does not belong to you. How much trouble would you be in if you shot a scene in your own living room and after the crew left, your folks discovered that someone left gaffers tape (like duct tape) stuck to expensive wallpaper, spilled soda on the couch, tracked mud on the carpet, scratched an expensive table with a piece of equipment, burned a hole in a lamp shade from using a bulb with too much wattage, plugged too many lights into an outlet and popped a breaker which supplied the refrigerator(and never fixed it), broke an antique plate in the dining cabinet, left the back gate open and allowed the dog to run off, and ... Shall I go on or do you get the picture? These are the kinds of mistakes that cause lawsuits for real film companies. So there are certain rules that you follow when you are on location, whether it is your property or someone else's.

There are a lot of tricks for getting the lights up out of the way for shooting in a low ceiling situation that involve light holding devices which tape or nail to the wall or ceiling. Not a good idea, use light stands or figure something else out. Crews will not die of thirst. No drinks in the house because eventually they will put it down and someone else will knock it over. Trust me on this one.

People's homes and businesses do not have furniture which want to be converted to work benches and shelves for your crew's equipment. They did not buy furniture for your crew to sit down on just after they put that sharp screwdriver in their hip pocket. The crew can sit on apple boxes, blankets you've brought to put on the floor, or outside.

Have no more than one light plugged into an outlet and make sure you know where the breaker box is located so you can get to it quickly. Do not plug any light into the circuit powering the refrigerator.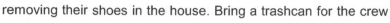

Bring blankets for the crew to walk on for the set area and ask them to get in the habit of removing their shoes in the house. Bring a trashcan for the crew to dispose of their trash as they create it. Most good art departments do this out of habit.

Once the location is shot out and the equipment is wrapped out, get in the habit of making an "idiot" check throughout the house for trash, moved furniture, company equipment, and a general walk through to inspect that all is back to order, including that large picture you removed from the wall and lost the nail that was holding it in place. The reason it is called an idiot check is because you would swear in court that you knew everything has been removed, only to find that you missed several items. Only an idiot does not check in the dumbest places to be sure nothing has been left behind. Be thorough. Most of the preceding is no-brainer kind of stuff, but amazingly, all has happen to my crews or my friend's crews.

For studio sets such as a sound stage on campus even more care should be taken by the crew to avoid traffic on the set. Art departments hate for the crew to 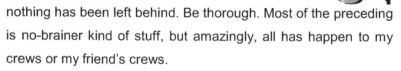 sit on furniture, fool around with props on the furniture, read magazines and books that are set dressings and so on. Hollywood studios go so far as to run tape across the set with signs that say: "Hot Set" That means stay off because items on the set like magazines or furniture locations have already been photographed and therefore will not match if they are moved. A good rule: Just stay off the set unless you have business to do like place a light, or place the camera.

There is a tendency on student projects to relax your level of professionalism to match that of the others. One person brings a drink cup onto a set, then someone else does, finally the rest think it must be okay, and everyone else does it. That's when someone spills the cup on the desk that has papers that are part of the storyline. Do not allow yourself to become a part of that trend. Maintain your own level of professionalism, regardless of what others do, you will be glad later when you are on a feature film set where the level of professionalism is high.

Preparing the Actors for Filming

Film acting is a difficult form of acting because of all the complications created by having a camera, lights, sound equipment and crewmembers in their line of sight while they are  acting in small spurts, sometimes without the benefit of the other actor to play off of in the scene. It is difficult for them to concentrate with all that is going on around them. I am a firm believer in giving your actors as much information as you can about the scene. How it will be photographed, where their focus should be, what scene happens before this one in the script, how far they should go in the script for this scene, how much movement they can make without going out of focus or out of frame, how to stay in their key light, on what line they should sit down or stand up, how far they can walk without creating lighting or camera problems, what tempo the scene should have, what level of intensity the scene needs, and where they may look to appear to be looking at the other actor not presently in the frame. Armed with this amount of information, they will give you their best performance and you will spend less time shooting takes.

Camera Rehearsal - Preparing the Company for Filming

To do this in the most efficient way, you need to have a walk thru. I like to invite the camera, lighting, sound and art department to come watch a rehearsal with the actors before any camera positions are decided or light fixtures are placed. The first run thru is that of the director explaining to the full company where the actors start and where they will be when they are finished with the scene. This tells the camera and lighting people what to expect in the way of movement. Then the actors give it a try and see if it feels natural for them. At that point, the crew can go about their work and the director can continue working with the actors on the scene. At some point the actors may want to be excused for hair and make up fine-tuning. If you are lucky enough to have stand ins, they move onto the set at this point and help lighting and camera people by indicating the location of the actors during the scene. Focus and lighting problems are worked out with the stand ins. The 1st A.D. judges when the crew is done and calls for the director and actors to take their places on the set. It is a smooth, professional way of respecting each department and allowing them to have a part in creating the realistic, natural and believable scene.

Chapter Sixteen

Preparing the Director for Filming

Directors come in all types, *unfortunately*. There are screamers, there are timid non-communicators, there are arrogant know-it-alls, and sometimes there are directors that have a  vision and are able to communicate that vision to their cast and crew without disrespect and without screaming at them like a child having a fit. I have, at one time or another, worked with them all, and I hope when I have directed, I have been the last type mentioned. I hope you will be the same. You will be more respected, more will be accomplished, and you will have more success. When people are under a lot of stress they make more mistakes not fewer, so screaming directors just increase the stress level on a set and that is poison for anything in the creative world. Fortunately, for student directors it is self-limiting. When working with unpaid student crewmembers, a screaming director will soon find himself or herself alone on the set. *I hope.*

Having observed student directors in action over the years, I have noticed certain common pitfalls that you can avoid. Directing is not a committee endeavor. There is only one director. Be <u>the</u> director. That does not mean you should ignore your cast and crew's input, but only you can judge whether their ideas are ideas you want to follow or your own. Everyone wants to help make the project a success, so sometimes if the director shows a lack of resolve about his or her convictions, the crew will bombard the director with: "Well, what if we do this..." Before long you will be swamped with so many suggestions that you will be spending all of your time explaining why their idea will not work for this particular situation. That is not the way the director should spend valuable set time. One way to avoid this bombardment from your crew is to not give them the impression that you are not clear about the direction you want to take. "I don't know how we should do this, what do you think?" Wrong! Instant death.

Have a plan, if you are not sure, do not say so. They will let you know if the scene is not working. Even beginning actors have a sense about the character they are playing and will often say something like: "I don't think she would say this." (Or "...say it like that") At that point you can easily say: "I'm not married to that dialogue, just the story. What would you be more comfortable saying?" When the actor tells you what that is, if you like it, you can say: "Okay, lets give that a try." After you have rehearsed the scene with the actor's new version, you can then decide if it works for you. If it does, say so and give them the credit. You may say to the actor: "Did that work better for you?" The actor will give you their commit and then you can reply: "Good, that works for me as well...Moving on!"

End of subject. You do not look like you do not know what you are doing. They do not feel that their input is of no value. And by moving on to the next phase without further discussion, you are not dwelling on it, which tends to give the situation too much power. If you do not like their way, suggest they do it both ways and you can both decide which to use later in order to save set time. Of course in editing, you use the one you like. Being a director is a people business, so if you are not good with people, learn to be.

The preceding explanation was included because I have seen

that situation played out over and over on student films and feature films where the director was a first time director or working with name stars who grind weak directors into a pulp on the first day. (I know this will come as a shock to your young minds, but some famous actors can be a real pain.) That scenario above seems to work better than set fights and power plays. As a famous Architect once said: "Less is more." In directing, that means do not let the cast or crew know everything you are thinking. Hold some things back so you alone know how all the pieces fit. The famous director, John Ford, was reported to have taken off his hat and placed it over the lens for portions of a scene he did not want the editor to use. If he was shooting a wide shot and he wanted the editor to use a close up for this part of the scene, the hat went in front of the lens so the editor had nothing to cut. The studio bosses hated him having that kind of control, but he know what he wanted and cut it in his head as he shot it. He also made the studios so much money they were reluctant to stop him from his annoying practice. If you think you would like to direct as a profession, you owe it to yourself to find books on some of the old time Hollywood directors, the stories are grand and the insight will help you form your own style.

Some of the best directors in Hollywood have one thing in common. Script notes. Some are pretty good artist and have drawings of the shots they want, most are not. Some hire storyboard artist to give them elaborate 'decks' of drawings for every part of every scene, most do not. Some fill the script with crib notes to the point that you can hardy read the printed script pages, most do not. All have some form of personal notes to which they refer as they shoot the scenes. I cannot imagine a good director neglecting his or her 'homework' by not making notes before arriving on the set. As a young wannabe director, I had the good fortune of working with an episodic TV director at Universal Studios. He would walk over to his script and refer to the frames drawn on the opposite side of the page of dialogue, study the frames, close the script book and we would continue. When I felt I knew him well enough to ask, I ask if I could see his script notes (He knew I was studying directing). Sure he said. I looked, there was nothing drawn in the frames except arrows pointing in various directions. They meant nothing to me and yet they seemed vital to him, because he would not shoot until he looked at these arrows. He saw my confusion and explained that he could not draw but he had been an editor for fourteen years so this was how he kept the scene straight in his mind. Decades later I have yet to figure out how that helped him. How it helped me was to realize that I really wanted to edit more than anything else. Something I greatly enjoy to this day. Some of the best directors started out as editors.

We have discussed the importance of the director being prepared by knowing the script and the shots that need to be photographed, and even some insights on dealing with the cast and crew while filming. As you can see there is a lot of preparation that goes into getting ready to film a scene for the director. It comes with the territory, just as a pilot has to file a fight plan, know the weather conditions, inspect the plane, go through the check list and make all the other arrangements before taking off. Would you like to fly with a captain that did not do those things each time he was ready to carry hundreds of people into the air? Good directors have a checklist as well. Let us consider the director's checklist:

☐ Know the script thoroughly for story content. Know the scenes and how they fit together.

☐ Make notes about the character. How they should act in this scene. What their subtext should be (What lies beneath).

☐ Make some kind of a storyboard indicating the framing and types of shots from establishing to close up. In other words, edit the scene on paper to make sure that all the angles you will want have been considered.

☐ Preplan your shot list, both the order you want to shoot and the kind of shots you will need to make the scene work. If you do not preplan those items you may shoot angles you do not need, wasting valuable time and money.

☐ Write detailed notes on the visuals involved to add the professional layers and textures that your project needs for yourself and the art department. Sit quietly and just think about the set or location and imagine how it should look. How does this scene fit with the last one and the next one. What kind of transition should the scenes make? A cut? A dissolve? Should there be a theme in the transition such as moving in on a lamp at the end of this scene and starting on a lamppost for the next? This one act, often makes the difference between amateurs and pros. Rent *Hoffa* directed by Danny De Vito and study the transitions he did from scene to scene. They are without a doubt some of the most beautifully conceived transitions ever made.

- ☐ Make notes for the camera and lighting department of your ideas for framing and mood. Are your angles subjective or objective? Will there be a lot of camera movement or locked down? What is the mood of the lighting to help tell the audience your story?

- ☐ Write notes as well for the sound department to alert them of any extra sounds you may need recorded. Example: "We need the sound of a dog barking in the distance, to which the actor reacts." Or you could need crickets, frogs or birds. Someone will need to get those items recorded. If you are on location for this scene, at sometime the sound person can go out an get those sounds while you are still on location. It requires you to make a note beforehand and remind them of it at the time, otherwise someone will be coming back later to record it.

When you arrive on the set and are bombarded with questions that each department has, you will already have a clear idea of what you want to see in this scene and will be able to answer  their questions succinctly. The best approach when you arrive on the set is to have your notes ready and meet with each department to map out what you expect from them before they have a chance to ask you first. A good starting point is with the camera and lighting department together. Then meet with the art department to give them some time to make any changes that you have thought of for this scene. The art department needs more lead time than the others so any 'heads up' you can give them the day before will help the set run more smoothly. The next group should be your actors which should include your 1st A. D. so that any notes that may include extras or other areas that the 1st A.D. controls can have time to make those arrangements. The final group can be the sound department. It will be their choice when will be the best time to collect wild tracks (as they are called) from the location. The crew is making so much noise that they may choose to record when the company is not making noise. Each location and set should have one minute of wild track recorded before you wrap. This gives your editor ambient sound unique to that 'room' to mix into the dialogue track to cover gaps created in stretching an edit of an actor's lines or pauses. A more detail explanation of this procedure will be explained in a later chapter on editing.

When the director is well prepared, there are fewer problem and surprises. It Is also contagious. The crew begins to pay more attention to performing their job in a more professional way and before long the crew and director begin running like a real film company. Of course, the above advice can also help feature film crews that have not had the benefit of this training, if they find that their company is not running as smoothly as it should. The team of filmmakers that use these time tested practices will find they enjoy the process a lot more and that the set is fun to be on with their fellow filmmakers.

Preparing the Assistant Director for Filming

For student projects, little is mentioned about the importance of the first assistant director, so few students realize the pivotal role this person plays in running the

company. The word assistant tacked on to anyone's title usually indicates that this person is second in command, having the same duties as the person above them in the chain of command. The assistant principal would naturally fill in for the principal in the principal's absence. That is not the job of the assistant director who is called the 1st A.D. The 1st A.D. is more like the Vice President of the United States of America. The President has a set of duties and the Vice President has his set of duties and only in the case of a national emergency would the Vice President take over the President's duties. So it is with the 1st A.D. in the overall structure of the duties.

Of course, the director is the boss, so to speak, but actually the director is concerned with the look of the project, the department heads and the actors. That is enough to keep the director busy.

The 1st A.D.'s job is the nuts and bolts running of the company. The 1st A.D. keeps the company working as quickly as possible to get the next shot ready, the next scene ready. It might be easier to just list all the duties of the first A.D. during the course of a day:

☐ Make sure all departments have arrived on location or at the studio at the proper time based on the call sheet which the 1st A.D. filled out and passed out to each member of the cast and crew the day before. If not, the 1st A.D. instructs the 2nd A.D. to start tracking down the missing member by phone or otherwise.

☐ Makes sure that the crew is correctly setting up the lights and camera equipment as rehearsed with the director. Clears the background of the shot from any crew equipment or unwanted items not wanted to be seen on camera.

☐ Makes sure the art department has all the set pieces, props, and scenery in place and ready to be filmed when the lights are set.

☐ Make sure that actors have arrived, gone to make up, hair, and wardrobe in a timely manner so that they can report to the set at the proper time.

☐ After blocking the scene with the director, places the extras and orchestrates how and when they will move within the background.

☐ Check to see that the sound department is in place and has a clear path to record the actors, and that the boom operator is not in the way of the camera or creating a shadow with the boom arm from the lights.

☐ Makes sure that the script supervisor agrees that there are no problems with dialogue (the actors are saying the correct lines) or with continuity. [See below for an explanation of the script supervisor's duties.]

☐ Asks if the camera department is ready, and when told that it is, calls for the camera to roll, followed by calling for the sound to roll. When they announce that they have "speed", the director will call for action. Once the 1st A.D. calls for the camera to roll, he or she hands control over to the director. Only the director should call for "Cut". From the time the 1st A.D. hands things over to the director until the director calls "cut", the director controls the action. Often, the 1st A.D. will silently cue the extras if they have different 'action' start points within the scene. This is usually when the background action has points when they should enter the frame.

The Importance of the 1st A.D.

In a lot of ways the 1st A.D. runs the company, not the director. This is to allow the director more focus on the actors and the action at hand. A good 1st A.D. is very valuable to the smooth running of a film  company, and serves an important role in making sure that work is progressing in a timely way.

When I first got into the business, I worked on "Kojak" at Universal Studios a few times. It was new to me and I could not figure out how the 1st A.D. knew just when the director was ready for the 1st A.D. to call for the camera to roll. The two had worked together enough to nonverbally know when that magic time was, or some other method I was unable to detect. One thing for sure about Universal, they move quickly and efficiently. They do not waste time. Any time.

Years later, after working both as a 1st A.D. myself and directing my own feature, I discovered their secret from those years before. There *was* no nonverbal communication, no secret hand signal. It was the knowing of the 1st A.D. that the director was finished instructing the actor, or camera operator, or whatever the delay was, and that it was time to get things moving. And here is an inside secret for 1st A.D. s of the future. There is a time, and no one knows when that point of time has arrived, that everything is quite ready to go. The camera is ready, the lighting is ready, the actors are waiting, the director is waiting. All are ready, but they do not <u>know</u> that the others are ready. So everyone is standing around talking while they wait for whomever was the hold up, only there is no longer a hold up. So only the 1st A.D. can seize the moment and get the company moving to start the next take. That takes savvy and alertness on the part of the 1st A.D. to keep the company moving. That is why I could not see what the 1st A.D. saw on *Kojak* all those years before. The 1st A.D. was seeing that everyone was standing around, waiting on each other. This is a valuable lesson to learn about the job of the first assistant director. Tough job, but a lot of fun. Thankless, but very rewarding, even if you are the only one who knows what a good job you have done for the company.

Another unsung hero is the script supervisor. This job would be considered a luxury on a student project and possibly unnecessary for shorter length projects. A necessity on feature length projects. There are a number of reasons  for having a script supervisor on the set at all times. The script supervisor:

Logs the takes as each scene is shot, noting details such as camera angle (Wide shot, medium, C.U.), what actors had lines, how far into the scene the take continued, any problems worth noting, if the director liked the take, and continuity of the scene. In the film industry this means what exactly happened during the scene such as the actor lit a cigarette on the word..., or the glass was left half full. All of these minuscule details are possible matching problems if ignored. With today's technology and film companies using video taps from the camera, it is easy to roll back to check for continuity, but it is a lot faster to just ask the script supervisor what happened. A good script supervisor is a valuable asset to the company, a bad one will bury you.

Chapter Seventeen

The Visual Dialogue

Art Directors come from all types of backgrounds. Some from architectural backgrounds, such as myself, some from interior design, some from art schools, and some from working their way into the  business anyway they could. The art director or production designer as they like to be called on big budget projects, create the visual dialogue that helps tell the story to the audience. On student projects, having an art director might be considered an unnecessary luxury. Let us consider for a moment why that might not be the case. This consideration will be multileveled.

As you have already discovered in this progression of studies, you have broken down into small groups of film companies. You have helped other students by being the camera operator on their project, they have helped you by recording sound for you. What is beginning to emerge in this swapping of duties, is your discovery that you like directing over camera work, or you like editing better than other jobs, and so on.

Student Feature Films

Once you have done several of these class projects you will began to discover just what it is in the film business that you want to do, if anything. Decades ago when I was in film

school there was no concerted effort to create new, young art directors, or art departments for that matter. As student projects grew in complexity and budget, we needed someone to take care of certain necessary aspects of the visual background maybe but that was about it. Some of our film projects verged on being student feature films so we are not talking about five to ten minute 'class projects' and there was a market in which to sell those films we created.

The technology emerging today in video is seeing a rebirth in those possibilities. What will hold back these student films from commercial release, if anything, will be poor acting and poor visuals. In a later chapter we will discuss acting, for now let us focus on visuals. So the possibility exists that your student project may see the light of day as a feature film?

Definitely.

Why?

Because there is a monster out there devouring product faster than it can be produced, called cable TV, or satellite TV, or internet direct TV, or whatever name it goes by today. The point is, people want more and there are more and more  avenues to the end user than ever before. It will not be diminishing anytime soon. Your product has as good a chance as anyone else's of finding its way to the consumer. A good example of this is the rise of two young men, Matt Damen and Ben Affleck. Their first film was shot on a shoestring because they just wanted to get out there and do something. They now have won Oscars for their writing in "Good Will Hunting" and continue to make outstanding films. Their careers could never have been launched as quickly as they were without their "student" project. "The Blair Witch Project" created the same kind of notoriety for its principal participants.

You may do it as well. There have been a number or student projects that stepped their creators through the door because they showed potential, but were not professional enough to be released as shot. The studios remade them with a bigger budget and professional craftspeople, sometimes with the original filmmakers in key positions, sometimes stolen from them. (Good luck suing a major studio.)

The job of the filmmaker is to create realism to the degree that the audience forgets that they are watching a film. This is called "suspension of disbelief". (Talk about a double negative!) Or not destroying your belief that it is really happening. The art department is a key player in creating this level of realism. How does the art department do that? Details.

The Art of Details

Over a couple of decades I observed art departments from within and without, taking an active role in the design of sets for high budget films and seeing their creation from a vantage point of other departments and seeing what the art department did with no  budget to speak of. In all of those experiences there was a common denominator, and that was the level of details that the art department provided in each of those projects.

For the average viewer of television or movies, little attention is paid to what is going on in the background consciously, but subconsciously our brains are processing the visual information and making an on-going evaluation of whether or not we believe what we see on the screen. Red flags come out when our brains say: "This does not look real."

It is interesting to contrast what was an acceptable level of realism in the past with what we expect today. Audiences in the thirties readily accepted the original *King Kong* with its jerky stop frame animation of the 'doll' gorilla, today we would laugh at its surrealistic attempt to create such a beast from toy models. Compare that with Steven Spielberg's *Jurassic Park* trilogy with its computer generated beasts. The art keeps getting more realistic with each new project. We keep pushing the envelope.

If you look at an original episode of "Star Trek" you will see William Shatner as Captain James T. Kirk, standing on the bridge of the *Enterprise* or in engineering. We accepted in those days, the painted cardboard tubes that were suppose to be some kind of a warp drive device. Contrast the starkness of that art direction with the later versions of the series with Patrick Stewart as Captain Picard and the two story engineering deck designed by a later art department.

There is a higher level of sophistication in the latter. That sophistication comes from more detail. It is not accurate to say that the level of sophistication comes from the use of more modern elements, or availably of more interesting products, because there have been a number of films that were period films predating the late sixties *Star Trek* series that used less sophisticated elements and still had a more interesting visual look. All of this comes from details. *Dr. No,* the original James Bond movie of the early sixties, had an underground facility that comes to mind as an example of a film that predated *Star Trek* with more 'gloss'.

Bringing this concept to a student level, let us examine how you can bring that level of cinematic texturing to your level of budget and understanding.

Countless movie stories have centered on the abandoned warehouse. There is a good reason for this, of course. It is a cheap and easy thing to find. No matter how it was left, it is probably perfect for what you want because it has *inherent texture*. The same for an abandoned or dilapidated old barn. Its own inherent texture is just what we would expect to find in such

a place. From rusted pitchforks to horse shoes nailed over a door. In a generic way, the same could be said for just about

any location you might choose, such as a living room or an office suite.

The more we move toward the generic, the less we have inherent texture. At this point, your art department begins to build texture into the location or set through set dressing. An example might be a generic bedroom is converted to a teen boy's room with sports car posters, model's posters, trophies and of course clothes thrown in every direction. All the things that speak to the audience in visual dialogue says this is a teenage boy's room, this happens through the art of details. It is the level of detail and

the willingness of your filmmaking team to include these minute details that determines the realism of your final visual product. In all likelihood, we are fast approaching a time when the salability of the project will be determined by the level of visual sophistication of the filmmakers, not the equipment budget

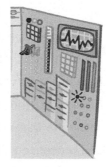

they have at their disposal.

The key to finding this inherent texture is through research of the location type. That is, what does a control room for a power station look like? For example, or what does the city morgue or autopsy room look like? In the case of the latter, you might discover that a portion of an autopsy room is not unlike the kitchen in a school lunchroom. Stainless steel metal tables, freezer doors, cabinets on the walls. The only visual problem might be the unsightly stove on one side of the room. A simple flat (a painted scenery piece that looks like a wall), painted the same color as other walls and placed in front of the stove, and you have converted the kitchen into a morgue. A few dressing pieces added on the flat such as charts of human anatomy, bulletin boards with office memos and busy work on them and you have a believable city morgue. Convincing the school to let you make the change for one night is the real trick. So one key component that your art department brings to the project is the ability to see, not what is there, but what *could* be there with a few small changes that look like much bigger changes on camera.

The Art of Camouflage

The basic aspects of film design deal with the elements that make up the frame. They include: Tone(value), contrast, perspective, focus, color(hue), texture and movement within the frame. These aspects are viewed  and processed by everyone who watches a film, everyone who watches a film also largely ignores them. After all, unless they are a film critic, the only interest a person has, is to be entertained. We all catch ourselves doing subconscious acts while concentrating on some other task. A woman might check her make up while driving on a busy freeway; a guy might watch a ball game while talking on the phone or tap our fingers for no reason at all. Our brains, like our computers are constantly multitasking, in the case of our brains, it is visual and sensual information. With all of this going on around us it is easy to trick the brain unto believing it has the whole picture when it  has only part. Magicians use this to their advantage all the time. Do you really believe he sawed her in half? Produced a <u>real</u> helicopter on stage behind a small screen in just a few seconds? In film school a banter that went around all the time was: "The camera never lies!" One person would say, then another would chime in: "It lies twenty-four times a second!" We never decided which was true. In this age of computer animation, I think we have the answer, finally. The camera lies <u>thirty</u> times a second. Do you really believe there were thousands of extras in the big scene? That a CGI dinosaur's tail could knock a real truck over? If your answer to these questions is a resounding no, then you are ready to understand how to dissect a film or video frame into smaller components to create such illusions.

The visual Frame
Every frame in its most basic division, has tone. What is tone? Tone or 'value' if you have an art background, in its most simple explanation, is the shades of gray that make up a picture. Since almost all video and film is done with color, it should be

explained that colors have a value as well. Yellows have lighter tone or value than dark blues or dark greens. In the old days of black & white filmmaking, the actual sets and wardrobe certainly were of some color, although the

Low Contrast

film was only able to record its tone or value as a shade of gray.

The frame has contrast. Contrast is the difference between light and dark, or the difference between light and the absence of light. When people tell me how much they liked the old black and white movies of the forties, I chuckle and wonder if they ever consider the fact that they were not black and white as much as they were just shades of gray. This is the essence of contrast. Without contrast, everything in the frame would look as if we were looking through a thick fog or through black, murky water. We must have contrast in order to have a picture that the audience can discern the elements that make up the image on the screen. Contrast unlike tone, is a comparison between the light to the dark.

Examples of Flat and Perspective Framing

The frame has perspective in order for us to sense that the image is real and not a flat painting. As mentioned in the chapter on camera framing, you enhance the perspective by your choice of framing or you destroy the perspective.

An Example of Excellent Composition and Visual Focus

The frame has focus whether that is your intent or not. It is important to learn how to judge where the focus of your framing is so that you may determine whether or not what is focused is what you intended to be the focus of your framing. This is of course, visual focus or interest, not the softness or sharpness of the lens.

There is color and texture within the frame and this is one of the most often ignored aspects of the student frame.

Textures

The point and shoot attitude, short attention span of the student tends to disregard the significance of both color and texture of the frame.

We understand color even if we do not know how to use it. Different colors have a different emotional response in the audience's mind. In a later chapter we will take a closer look at this subject. Texture has a more subtitle effect on the audience.

A smooth plaster wall has one texture, a course brick exposed mortar wall has another. A concrete block wall in a jail cell has one texture, a wood paneled wall with paintings has another. Both give vital visual information to the audience.

Movement within the frame also creates a visual aid to the perspective of the frame. The subject moving within the frame and changing size as it moves away or comes closer to the camera helps the audience sense the three-dimensional space.

These are all tools that the filmmaker has at his or her disposal to enhance the visual experience. To bring all of this into context of art direction, let us imagine a particular film design problem as an example.

Realistic illustrations of likely possibilities in your near future always have more impact than far fetched situations you may never encounter. So let us say that you are fresh out of film school and land a contract to produce a promotional video for a national manufacture of some type of widget. [if you have never heard of this term before, a "widget" is a nondescript item meaning something that is made. There is no product or device actually called a widget.]

Your First Big Job

This widget has been made the same way as it was when the company was founded in the early twenties by the grandfather of the man who has hired you. One of the themes important to  your client is that this company has been around for a long time and therefore garnered the public's trust and reputation for dependability. The client wants to see re-enactments of his grandfather at work in the factory stamping out this widget on a big machine. And of course, as always, there is no budget to build sets and hire studios in which to shoot this twenties style set.

With your art director along, you ask for a tour of the factory. It looks like it was built last year, complete with mercury vapor and fluorescence lights, stark white, clean walls, picture windows looking out on the factory floor from modern offices above, and hazard warning yellow and black stripe paint on the pristine concrete floors noting safe walking areas. Even a neon sign on the wall promoting safety first. And yet there is hope. In one corner sits one of the original stamping machines, the owner keeps it in working condition as a tribute to his grandfather's hard work in building a great company.

Your art director makes a few quick sketches and takes a couple of digital camera pictures from possible camera angles for the re-enactment scenes. Back at the office, it looks impossible. The neon sign, the white walls, mercury vapor lights. All you can see is a fortune being spent to dress the existing location to look twenties style or worse, having to haul heavy machines to a studio to create it.

The Illusion of Details

The art director uses rough one by twelve lumber from a used lumberyard to create a column for the frame right foreground to block sight of the neon sign on the wall. On this column he places a metal conduit and a  surface mounted light switch to help sell the fact that this is a column holding up part of the building. On the wall behind the stamping machine he places vertical planks of wood siding, common for that era. In the middle of that wall, he places a plastic three-inch pipe that has been painted to look like cast iron, old and partially rusted. Tacked onto this false wall are old style calendars, antique posters (rented not bought) some more metal conduits and outlets with old style plugs, a wooden shelf with an old coffee maker and cups on it (From a thrift store). He places a large black plastic tarp, draped high above the set to block that nasty blue mercury vapor lighting pouring into the set area. The actual original stool in which his grandfather sat is found and brought back into service. An actor with a great looking mustache is put in coveralls and a plaid shirt you would not be caught dead in, and lit with warm gelled lights. Your art director brings a fog machine or smoke cookie to the shoot and smokes up the 'set' so that there are streaks of "sun" light coming through what must be a large twenties style factory window just out of frame, complete with shadow bars of the window hitting the actor's shoulders as he stamps out the widget we are promoting. A soft diffusion filter on the camera and the illusion is complete. Total set cost, probably less than a hundred dollars. Value of your art director, *priceless*.

These kinds of scenarios are being played out everyday in small production companies like the one you may find after this course. Sometimes it is ingenious, sometimes it is pitiful, the way that these illusions are created for the camera. Armed with the information given in this chapter and others you will be much better equipped to be ingenious rather than pitiful. It is all a matter of looking at what could be, rather than what is there in frame.

Class assignment: Create a two-minute industrial film about a company real or imagined, based on the opportunities that you have available to you.

Notes:

Chapter Eighteen

Understanding Promotional Productions

People hardly find out you are interested video production before they are calling you to shoot their weddings, bar mitzvahs, anniversaries and maybe a local commercial or promotional video for a relative's company. Occasionally they may  actually pay you for the services you render. Only you can decide how much of this social abuse you want to endure before putting your foot down and start charging a scheduled fee for your services.

More than likely, your first venture into producing promotional videos will be for a friend or a relative on a more personal basis. Chapter twenty-six will deal with the more professional aspects of promotional videos. In this chapter we will consider the basics involved in your first productions. Any professional venture with outside clients, even if they are relatives, should begin with a conference with the prospective client to determine exactly what they want and what they expect from you.

In this first meeting you should find out the following:

☐ What is the purpose of this presentation?

☐ Where will it be shown?

☐ What time frame is involved?

☐ What is your expected budget range?

☐ What does the client want the video presentation to say overall?

☐ How long does the client think the video should last?

☐ How much use does the client expect to get from this

presentation?

☐ Does the client have a need for different versions of this presentation?

Once these answers have been discussed, the following group of questions may need further examination:

☐ Is the purpose of the presentation for broadcast or in-house use such as a point of purchase video explaining some benefit to the customer?

☐ Does the time frame allow adequate production time?

☐ Is the client's expected budget range realistic?

☐ What the client wants the video presentation to say is within the scope of what you can provide?

☐ Is the client's expected running time realistic in terms of cost and script?

☐ If the client needs different versions of the presentation, will there be extra funds to allow for this extra work on your part?

Some of these questions may not be pleasant for you to ask when you first get started, but you will soon find that business people appreciate an up-front approach. They will more likely feel you are capable of  doing the work if you are also professional about the fees and time involved. **No** project that involves a set payment to you for your services should begin without a payment in advance for a percentage of the overall work to be done.

Hands On Experience

Mock class presentations with the teacher or instructor as the client is a good way of getting practical experience in the field of interest. Since the teacher has many in a class doing the same assignment, a handout of the requirements for this mock presentation will suffice, in lieu of personal conferences.

These first presentations should be no longer than two minutes in length, with music only as a background, without voice over or dialogue. The presentations will be a visual exercise only. Graphics on screen to clarify a point are acceptable.

Lesson Number One:

The first video should be a video on the proper way to install a printer for a computer, including checking the ink system and paper supply for non-computer wise individuals. This DVD would be given to customers buying a new system.

Lesson Number Two:

The next type of video should be a video on the step-by-step procedures for installing a DVD player for a television and cable system. This should include clock setting. [This can be faked in class using a school DVD player.]

Lesson Number Three:

Option 1: A video for people who do not have the education or maybe background skills to properly fill out a deposit slip for banking. [Don't laugh, the author once made such a video for a national banking system.]

Option 2: A video for people who need help understanding how to access information on the web for the first time.

These presentations should be presented to the class and critiqued for clarity and understandability without the use of dialogue or voice over in the video.

Notes:

Chapter Nineteen

Understanding Commercial Productions

Commercial Productions come in different scales, from a small own local business to a multinational corporate sponsor of sporting and television events. The average commercial runs for thirty seconds, which is nine hundred frames in which

to tell the sponsor's story or get out their message, they can be produced on a shoestring, or cost millions of dollars.

The big budget advertising agency which charge a sponsor or client fifteen percent for their agency fee, spend thousands of dollars of their client's money on focus groups, psychological studies of people, research on the product impact on the public, and other studies to gleam how to best get the results in advertising for their client.

With the advent of the computer animation systems being more available to the general public, it is now within the reach of one person to produce breathtaking *spots,* as they are called in the industry, for a local client or national agency.

The old adage: *A professional is someone who makes something very hard look easy*, is never more true than here. Making award winning commercials (The award is called a Cleo) requires great attention to detail in bringing everything together in only nine hundred frames and one can spend hundreds of thousands of dollars to do that.

The Concept

It all begins with a concept, an idea that will grab the attention of the public and force them to watch the spot not once, but over and over. We all have our favorites, from dogs,  cats, raccoons, and talking cars to computer animated personalities. So much money can be spent on a concept that may not work, that large agencies test their concepts in a number of ways and to different degrees of detail.

As you embark on a course of learning these basic concepts in advertising, you will be doing the same thing that agencies do on a day to day basis. Your concept should start by asking yourself a number of questions that begin with:

☐ What is the purpose of this commercial?

☐ Where will it be shown?

☐ What does the client want the commercial to say to the public?

☐ How long does the client think the commercial should air?

☐ How much business does the client expect to get from this spot?

☐ Does the client have a need for different versions on the same theme?

A paragraph in the last chapter on promotional videos about working with real clients bares repeating:

☐ Some of these questions may not be pleasant for you to ask when you first get started, but you will soon find that business people appreciate an up-front approach. They will more likely feel you are capable of doing the work if you are also professional about the fees and time involved. **No** project that involves a set payment to you for your services should begin without a payment *in advance* for a percentage of the overall work to be done.

Even with the answers to the basic questions, you are still only at a concept stage without any real idea of what you want to present to the client as an ad campaign. Brainstorming ideas for a clever new commercial is something that highly paid old pros still pull their hair out trying to do day after day.

The following group of questions may help find that clever new idea for selling their product or service:

☐ Is the purpose of the spot to show some benefit to the customer?

☐ Is the client's expected budget realistic?

☐ What the client wants the spot to say is something you can provide?

☐ If the client needs different versions of the spot, how will the spots run? At the same time, one after another, or during certain seasons of the year?

Hands On Experience

With the teacher or instructor as the client as in the last chapter you will be able to get a better feel for how to begin making commercials. As before, a handout of the requirements for this  mock commercial will suffice, although your ideas should be presented to the teacher in storyboard form of your concept along with personal conferences, followed by a class presentation just the way an agency would 'pitch' their idea to a group of corporate clients. It is a good way to get some valuable experience in front of people. You will learn by watching each other and pick up fresh ideas from each other as you all make your presentation.

These spots will be thirty seconds in length, with music, with voice over or with dialogue as required by the concept. Graphics on screen to clarify a point are acceptable and encouraged. Computer animation is acceptable as only a part of the concept.

Practical Projects for Real World Preparation

Lesson Number One:

Option 1) The client's business is a store in a mall offering a close out sale.

Option 2)The client's business is a service provided to consumers.

Lesson Number Two:

Option 1) The client's business is a national product supplier.

Option 2) The client is a person seeking a national political office.

Lesson Number Three:

Option 1) The client's business is a national service business. (Insurance, etc.)

Option 2) The client is a national franchise.

These spots should be presented to the class and critiqued for clarity and freshness of concept for each phase of the process.

Chapter Twenty

Advanced Editing Techniques

This text would not be complete without a detailed chapter on advanced editing techniques, based on countless documentaries, promotional films, feature film and music video work. For most of that time, the machine of choice was not a computer but  a flatbed Moviola, a film splicer, and synchronizer with rewinds. There is a smell of film fresh out of a film can that sadly you will never know, unless you become a negative cutter. As more and more projects, such as George Lucas' work, are not even being shot on film, the chances that you will ever experience that by-gone era become less with each passing day. What is constant in this ever changing world of editing, is the use of the edit within a film or video presentation. Those rules and requirements never change.

Unobtrusive Cutting

The first rule of skillful cutting is to make an edit unobtrusive. If an edit calls attention to itself the audience will lose its concentration on the action of the scene. If your job as an editor is to cut music videos or news stories  for the nightly news, it may take you a long time to understand the importance that each edit has on the natural flow of a scene. If you are cutting a dramatic scene in a fictionalize story, it will jump off the screen at you the first time you make a bad edit.

You may not know why at that point in your learning curve, but you will know something does not look like it does in the movies. What is that, that caused the bad edit? The answer is the edit was not unobtrusive. It was at the wrong moment or it was the wrong choice to go from that shot to the one you chose. How do you learn the right choice to make?

There are some considerations that you need to understand if you are going to avoid these kinds of mistakes:

☐ In cutting from one shot to the next, any material that is present in both shots must match perfectly. If an actor is holding a glass of water in a wider shot, and you cut to a closer shot, the relative position of the glass must match. If that action includes movement, such as raising the glass to drink, the flow from one shot to the next must match exactly, otherwise the glass will jump back in space or jump forward in space as it moves, depending whether you cut too far ahead of the action in the incoming shot or too late.

☐ In cutting from one shot to the next, the image position within the frame should match. The eye should not be jerked about to find the next image. (That is why MTV editing is so painful for me to watch.) If there is movement such as the subject moving from left to right on the screen, the incoming shot should have this same smooth flow of action.

☐ There should be a continuity of idea between shots. For example, if the outgoing shot is of a jogger running, if the incoming shot is of the jogger standing still, there is a loss of the sense of flow from one shot to the next.

☐ It is important that the lighting between the shots not have any glaring mismatch. Sunny day to overcast or bright room to darker room from cut to cut is a noticeable problem for the viewer. This is also true of color changes as well, of course. So the first job of the editor is to choose from all of the material shot to find these few pieces of material that work together to form a cohesive edited scene. But all we have done at this point is the most basic type of decision making that an intern with a sharp eye could accomplish. Editing is so much more.

Rhythm of the Edited Scene

The length of the shots determines the rhythm of an edited scene, so the editor must always endeavor to cut the shot as short as possible. But what determines what is "as short as possible"? The answer is the shot content sets up its own expectation of the next cut. In other words, the audience has rhythm even if you don't. As guilty as most beginners are about holding a shot too long, it is equally annoying to the audience to have the shot taken away too soon, before they can absorbed the visual content of the edit, be that visual information only, or emotional information presented by the actor. This is called the *completion of the action*. There is a fine line here to be considered in editing, so fine that some take years to fully grasp this understanding, other never get it. Twice in my life, I tried to teach editing to two people that I could still be tutoring and they would not have it yet. But by the same token, I have tried on occasions to learn how to play the drums. I never got it. I doubt I ever would, and that is okay, just as it is okay if not everyone can understand editing.

A skillful editor knows how to cut a moment before the completion of the action, which depends on the understanding the editor has about the audience's ability to know how the action will be completed, and will accept the quick cut as a means of moving the action along. This is the removal of the <u>inessential</u> in editing. So we cut every shot as short as possible, once the essence has been comprehended by the audience, since we can not push beyond their limit of concentration. At the same time we hold the shot long enough to match their attention span.

This forced pacing of the audience's experience is not unlike what a comic does on stage as he or she tells a joke and gets a laugh. If they rush on to the next joke before the audience's laughter peaks, the audience will miss the set up for the next joke. If the comic waits too long they become restless, waiting for the next joke. This timing of the audience's interest by the comic is like the editor holding the shot just the right amount of time. A film that displays this art to the greatest extent is, without question, *Sleuth*, starring Sir Laurence Olivier and Michael Caine.(1972) I can not imagine how you would find this gem but it will be worth your effort if you can. This tour-de-force for both men (if that is possible for *both* to have) originated as a stage play brought to the screen by director Joseph Mankiewicz. The entire story is played out with only the two actors. For reaction shots, the editor cuts to life-size mannequin type clowns and figurines. The amount of time that the editor holds on these figurines is just the right amount of time to give them the life needed to make that world seem real. The moments that the editor chooses to cut to these figurines is also exactly right. The plot twists and story are too good to ruin for you in case you are able to see it. It is a must see film for any one wanting to understand the art of editing.

Shot Selection

The initial process for the editor is the shot selection from the material available. From the several takes available, certain decisions must be made first on a technical basis, then to the  aesthetical. The technical reasons are because some shots may be out of focus or there is a mismatch of the action. This unfortunate set of circumstances often leads to not being able to use the actor's best performance.

Once this process has been completed, the editor can begin looking for the *soul of the shot*. This means trimming off the front of the shot and the tail of the shot until all that is left is the bare essentials of the shot. In the old days of work-print cutting on film, if I cut a take a few frames short I had to piece those frames back on the work-print with splicing tape. A painful job, thankfully you will never experience, but it does teach you a few things like make sure you want to cut just there, and the patience to take the time and effort to go back and re-cut it because it will make it right if you do. Years later, I had the benefit of a Grass Valley computer editor and state-of-the-art Sony Betacam SP VTRs to make those changes in seconds, and that was linear editing. Now we have non-linear computer editing. This gives you a wonderful way to learn the craft with few restrictions to slow you down.

Determining the Order of Shots

The main restrictions of linear editing over non-linear editing is the choices that must be made with finality. Many a time I had to go back and rebuild a whole sequence of shots because one of the first ones was a few frames short or long. The beauty of non-linear editing allows you to change those shots at any time during the edit process. I think this ultimately will shorten the learning curve for beginning editors. More importantly, there are aesthetical reasons for choosing the order of the shots to use in any one scene.

Traditional shot arrangement has determined the beginning shot of a sequence in most feature film and industrial filmmaking. That is of course, the establishing shot, sometimes called the long shot. One of the first things the audience is asking subconsciously as a new sequence begins is: "Okay, where are we?" The long shot gets that out of the way so that the audience's attention can be focused on what the filmmaker wants to say cinematically.

Breaking with Tradition

There are times that you want to break with this tradition in order to disorient the viewer, or hold off for some reason, the visual information they are seeking. The *okay, now where are we* question can be an editor's device for holding or even building the viewer's interest. It should be clear that this non-traditional approach does have an effect on the audience. You will also discover that by skipping this establishing shot at the beginning there often is no appropriate place to give this visual information to the viewer later in the scene without breaking the rhythm you create as the scene progresses. In other words, don't break the rules unless you have good reason. Don't re-invent the wheel.

Determining the order of shots is usually a function of following the script first and then determining the best possible angle based on material supplied to you. If you begin as an editor and then progress to directing you will have an entirely different approach to directing. You will be cutting in your head as you shoot and you will be creating more shots while shooting to cover yourself in editing. You will also have a better sense, while shooting, as to whether you have the best take or not. You hear and see your actors as an editor, not as a director. There is a big difference there that I am at a loss how to explain. You just know when you have it and you know when you do not have it. Perhaps it comes from years in the editing room, listening to actors.

If you watch a lot of films closely, you will discover that sometimes while one person is talking, the editor has chosen to hold on the actor not talking. This decision on the part of the editor has a number of effects on the audience. The first of course is the pacing of the scene cutting, the second is the control the editor has on what the viewer's attention will be. You will notice that this choice is usually to hold on the *close up* of the non-speaking actor, and not a medium or wider shot. The reason is the editor is focusing on what the actor is *thinking*. That is not usually expressed with a wide shot. We need to be in close to sense what the actor is reflecting on what the other actor is verbalizing.

Action Sequences

In cutting the action sequence, the editor has the most control over the order of the shots and their length. Action sequences require many set ups from several angles, creating a very high ratio of footage shot to footage that will be finally used in the edited master. When you consider several takes from multi-camera angles, the ratio of forty to one is not uncommon, when considering the final running time may be even less that the length of one take not more. The average low budget film shoots in excess of ninety thousand feet to produce a finished film of about eight thousand feet (at ninety feet per minute). *Jaws*, Steven Spielberg's first major film, is reported to have shot more than two hundred and fifty thousand feet. That is a lot of footage for an editor to plow through to find just the right take of just the right length. In planning the cutting of an action sequence, the editor must consider the tempo that is being created by the edited sequence as it progresses. If that tempo is erratic or inconsistent, it will show in the final product. The advice given in chapter six on cutting on the beat, does not apply in action cutting. There are times that a cut longer than twenty frames looks absolutely dead in the water, whereas sixteen frames or twelve frames 'sells' the shot just right. There is no formula that allows an easy shortcut to action cutting. Each shot must be judged in and of itself for its required running time. The tempo is developed through the series of shots that build the excitement of the moment. If you use an expensive DVD player that is capable of (jitter free) freeze frame by frame analysis of a rented movie from the video store and use it to count each frame in a fight scene or car chase, you will be amazed at how short some of the cuts are. I was surprised to discover that one Arnold Schwarzenegger action film had cuts of only six frames in one sequence. I had to admit to myself, in studying the sequence, that any longer would have killed the pace and the tempo. I still enjoy learning by watching other's work. It is a journey, not a destination that you should begin as well.

The Montage

The montage sequence is a series of shots blended together to create a scene that may or may not have been shot all at one time. The most typical montage sequence that everyone has seen at one time or another is the romantic montage where two people meet and fall in love. We see them buy food at a open air market, take a stroll hand in hand by a lake, kiss with the sun setting in the background, and you know the rest. It is usually set to some appropriate music.

This is a classic example of how the viewer is willing to dismiss the inessential. In this case, it is a prolonging of a series of scenes of the couple meeting at the market with dialogue, a stroll with sweet nothings being said, them commenting on the beautiful sunset, and so on. We accept that they got to know each other and foll in love and said a bunch of things along the way. The montage states all of this "getting to know each other" in a simple group of shots that are usually dissolved from one to another in a matter of seconds instead of minutes. This is the removal of the inessential. Someone once said that every good film has a montage. Perhaps that is another way of saying good movies don't bore you to death with unnecessary dialoged scenes.

The Montage Decisions

The question becomes how do you decide how to group these shots together. In film school we use to say: "If you can't solve it, dissolve it." Sadly today it would be more accurate to say: "If you can't solve it, flip it, spin it, morph it, explode it, or digitize it." We have gotten a little out of hand with the special effects transitions. The *If you can't solve it, dissolve it* phrase came from the editing problem of not being able to make two shots work together so you just dissolved from one to the other. If that is your only criteria, then any two shots will blend together. Editing should be much more sophisticated than that in determining your shot sequence. So what are the elements of that decision making process?

We can break that down into some basic patterns to look for in the material the director has given to you from which you are to build the montage.

Let us begin by considering the raw footage we have for this montage. The order in which the sequences were shot does not have to matter, the location of this shot or that shot does not have to matter, the time of day does not have to matter, the time of year does not have to matter. You are free to pick any one of these factors to determine what will be your progression of shots or none of these.

Patterns of Choice

There is a pattern to the choice that you will make, and that should be based on content, form, idea or flow of motion. Progression of the montage based on *content* would be to choose shots based on some theme within the frame of the picture. Say, older cars to the latest version. Or short legged dogs to the tallest dogs. The content determines what the next shot in the sequence will be. Progression of the montage based on *form* would be to choose your shots based on the form of the subjects in the frame. A fence post to a pine tree to a tall redwood in a forest. Or a single book to a shelf of books to a library full of books.

Progression of the montage based on *idea* would be people

playing musical instruments, one after the other in a progression. Or factory workers, each one doing something different, but each progression showing that what they have in common is working very fast. Progression of the montage based on *flow of motion* is of course the easiest to imagine. What is difficult to do is have several shots moving left to right, then insert one going right to left. If the items are to be shown going both directions it is better to alternate them in an expected pattern of one in one direction and then one in the other. [Back and forth never really worked for me, it just looks badly planned.]

Ways to Create a Montage

So out of all the footage that has been presented to you, you now have several ways to create a montage. The experiences you have already had in making simple music videos in previous chapters will be of service to you as you judge how to create the montage. Unlike action cutting, a montage needs to be cut on the beat if you are fortunate to have the music score before you start. If not, then plan to keep your shots in an order of equal length, in general. You may find that you want montage segments to be in the range of eight to sixteen seconds with dissolves in the range of two to four seconds in length. It all depends on the subject matter and the inherent flow of action within each shot. A montage of a car race would hardly work with sixteen second shots and four second dissolves. The tempo of the material will have its own pace and timing that will guide you into finding its 'groove'. Fundamentally, it does help to have the music laid down first because it sets your tempo for you.

Continuity

The transition from one sequence to the next is the way the storyteller is able to compress time in moving the story along. A simple example of this is when we see someone start to shut the car door in the driveway and cut to inside the house as they close the front door. We have compressed all of that inessential material of the car door being locked, walking to the front door, unlocking the door and entering. The question becomes how do you cut out all of the inessential and still maintain continuity?

There are two types of continuity that need to be explained here. One, there is the continuity mentioned above and there is the *within the scene continuity* that must be observed. The second might best be described this way: A car is racing around a race track. We see certain landmarks in the background that give us an idea of where the car is on the track, perhaps rounding the last curve before the straightaway. We cut to a reaction shot of a spectator watching with binoculars for a few seconds, then back to the race car. In cutting these shots together, as we cut back to the car it needs to be farther down the track the appropriate length that it would have moved while we were seeing the spectator. This is a relative thing and can be used to your advantage when needed to compress the time or expand it. Am I the only person that thought the final train scene in *Back to the Future III*, lasted a lot longer than the amount of track they had in the story? (Who cares, it was a great finale) That is an example of expanding the time frame continuity by inner cutting from one action to another.

Care must be taken not to push the envelop of believability in manipulating the natural time frame. If you have your hero seeing the timer on an explosion set to go off in fifteen seconds and he runs from the cave taking two minutes of action packed obstacles blocking his exit to get him out, you probably should consider a minor script rewrite and make that one minute on the timer because the audience will not buy it.

A scene in which you know the time frame has been monkeyed with and yet works, is the big climatic scene in *Goldfinger*, where Sean Connery is cuffed to the atomic bomb with seconds before it will go off. He tries desperately to shut It off. A military man approaches from three stories away as we watch the timer ticking down. Finally, the man shuts it off with only seconds before detonation. (Of course the timer stopped at 007.) The inner cuts from the military man approaching, and the timer ticking down have that type of continuity that is required to be believable to the audience.

The type of continuity mention first, the removal of the inessential, is more a matter of choice of the screenwriter, director and you as the editor as to how much of that you can compress a scene sequence. Those decisions are best made in the writing stage. Sometimes you can make those decisions in the editing stage if you feel the story is dragging because the inessential was filmed but is too tiring for the audience to watch to be included. Cutting it out will pick up the pace of the scene sequence.

The Language of Film and Video

The language of film was determined by millions of filmgoers long before you were born and have become a time honored tradition in filmmaking. Certain choices the editor makes have certain meaning to the audience. When you misuse these techniques in your editing, you are not creating a whole new exciting use of the techniques, you are simply misusing the ones that have long been established. If you do not know the correct meaning of a word you might misuse it in a sentence. Other people who know the correct meaning will not think you are more intelligent than they are and creating a whole new meaning to the word, they will simply think you are an idiot.

With this time honored tradition in filmmaking language, these following elements have a meaning that you as a beginning editor should be aware:

☐ Fade in- The fade in says to the audience that this is the beginning of a new scene or time in the story. Contrary to *MTV,* it does not belong in the middle of a music video without any previous fade out to match it.

☐ Fade out-This belongs at the end of a scene which says to the audience that this is the end of this time frame.

☐ Dissolve-This says that the time from one shot to the next is a compression of time. That something that would have been in between has been omitted.

☐ Swish Pan-Means while this was going on, this other thing happened, or a compression of time. The swish pan is seldom used any more.

☐ Wipe-The wipe or any other type of transition such as this means a compression of time. [Flip wipe, circle wipe, digitize, morph, explosion, etc.]

☐ Cut-No time compression, the scene is continuing without a time interruption.

Understanding Advanced Editing Techniques

Armed with these basic elements in editing you should have a better understanding of advanced editing techniques and use them in a professional way. Like most artistic endeavors, it is not the theory that makes it easy, but the practice that gives you confidence that you are proceeding correctly. The wonderful thing about the editing process is the fact that as you watch an edited sequence you will be able to see where you have made a mistake. You will be able to correct these mistakes as you go. In the beginning, you will make big mistakes that jump off the screen at you. Later, these will become fine, one or two frame mistakes that only you will be able to notice. After thirty plus years of editing I still make one or two frame mistakes, which I correct. Usually, students or friends watching me are not able to understand why I needed to correct the edit by one or two frames, because to them, it looked okay before. I have no answer for them except to say it is a matter of fine-tuning the edit rhythm and that one or two frame difference to me is a big one.

The one overriding rule that will make it all easier is to remember to have patience. If you rush the editing process, it will look sloppy an unprofessional. Take your time to get it right and it will surely outlive you with something you can be proud.

Class assignment: Create a two-minute montage from a rented video movie by transferring a scene sequence to your editing computer and then condense the action to a montage and set the action to music. As long as you do not charge for screening the edited material or sell the finished product, you will not be breaking any copyright laws.

Notes:

Part Three

Production

In this final section of the text you will learn the basics for professional filmmaking based on the Hollywood standard for marketable filmmaking. Not everyone is interested in such a pursuit, but it is important to apply professional standards to whatever filmmaking you decide to do whether that is a local television station, boutique production facility in your local area or part of a large staff in a regional production facility.

If you choose to do it all, there are basics contained within to help you get started in that direction. If your interest is more departmentalized you will find information on that as well, and in a broader sense, there is information that will help you understand the workings of those other departments with which you will be assisting. All of this will be of benefit to you as you make the transition from student to professional.

Filmmaking, unlike a number of other pursuits is more hands on practice than it is theory. For that reason, it is important to be observant of what is going on around you both in the class room and in the field, working. Such a text as this can not be appreciated without lab work in order to see those finer areas that can not be properly addressed in a textbook. Homework for this curriculum should be as much observation of the movies that have gone before as it is on movies that you will be working during the course. As you watch movies as part of the class work and on your own, you will learn to see how to make movies or how not to make movies. It is all part of the process. As a young doctor goes through med school to learn that discipline, so you will, as interns, learn the craft of making entertainment through on the job training.

Chapter Twenty-One

Cinema-verite'

Cinema-verite' is French for hand-held camera (in short). At a time when independent filmmakers used 16MM film as a acquisition medium, there was a movement called the underground film. This was not a  movement promoting films about mine workers. The underground film was a total disregard for the conventions of Hollywood and the studio system. The closest analogy today would be *gorilla filmmaking*, where what you shoot, no matter how rough it is, is what you get. It is important to discuss this type of filmmaking because with the advent of the digital video camera and the computer as an editing device, we are rapidly approaching a time when we will see a resurgence of this artistic and acceptable form of filmmaking due to the players involved, namely a group of, for the most part, inexperienced filmmakers.

The style is not without its serious drawbacks due to editing and continuity problems inherent with such a style. It does have its attractions, though, as seen by the fact that even Hollywood flirted with it in the early nineties with a show called "NYPD-Blue". Since Panavision cameras are quite heavy with all the options they can carry, it was decided to mount the heavy tripod and 35MM camera on a plywood platform which sat on a inner tube, this created an unstable, shaky camera situation that somewhat mimicked the shaky camera of the cinema-verite' style. The effect they wanted was a 'in your face', gritty, documentary style of hand-held realism.

Like the 'Emperor's new clothes', the producer was so well renowned that everyone thought it was ingenious. I think the show was probably outstanding from a writing and acting point of view. I say *think*, because I could never watch it because of the annoying shaky, darting to and fro, camera that jerked around so much, it took away from the story. Styles that call attention to themselves rank down there with MTV, in my opinion. I remarked to a friend who worked on the series, my annoyance with the style, to which he retorted that they had just won an Emmy for it. *Only in Hollywood.* (They had to give it to *some* show that year.)

Speed Filmmaking

The beauty of the cinema-verite' style is the attempt of the camera operator to shoot as steady a shot as possible, without the aid of a tripod to lock down the shot. The speed in filmmaking with this saving in set up time is remarkable. As you no doubt have guessed, this sounds a lot like the small hand held camcorder so popular today, and therefore the reason for explaining this style of filmmaking. What *NYPD* seems to have missed in resurrecting this style was the fact that the camera operator is not trying to shake the camera as *NYPD* did, but trying very hard to **not** shake the camera at all. The swish pans to another actor used in conjunction with this style were to make it all look unrehearsed and documentary. Like most things in Hollywood taken to the extreme, it gets lost and the style becomes blatantly dishonest, rather than truthful filmmaking. Their first clue should have been when they decided to mount a tripod on a inner tube to create a false shake. How honest is that?

As you consider gorilla filmmaking as a style for some project you may consider, there are certain things you will want to do. No matter how hard you try to hold the camera steady, you will have a lot of movement that you would not get with a tripod. The use of a hand-held shot tends to express a subjective point of view so care should be taken to keep the framing consistent with locked down shots. Editing is also a problem from a matching point of view. It is difficult to jump from one shaky shot to another. The inner cutting tends to exaggerate the movement problem. There are ways of avoiding these inner cutting problems through the use of shots that are from locked down tripods in between the hand-held shots. That's signals a sudden jump in shooting styles which gets away from the gorilla filmmaking look you wanted. One possible solution is to keep the camera zoomed out wide, which minimizes the feeling of movement and to frame shots wider than you might if the camera were locked down on a tripod. Some camcorders have an image stabilizing system built in to minimize the shaky framing look. All of these techniques will help and you may find that the cinema-verite' style works for you in telling your dramatic story.

Getting Back to Basics

Using two cameras to shoot each of your scenes can eliminate some of the problems mentioned above such as editing. Since the cameras usually do not have time coded sync capabilities, you will need to use a clapboard  slate to lock sync between the two or more cameras so that you will be able to edit shots from one camera to the other. It would be wise to test this technique along with your editing computer's ability to inner cut these two sources before launching a video feature.

In the old days before radio controlled, time code synced slate boards; a simple slate with a clapboard on top was used to sync the sound with the camera. This was done by closing the clapboard down on the top of the slate to produce a loud popping noise. The editor would then sync the sound on the film sound roll with the frame showing the picture on the picture roll of the slate just closing. Once those two events were matched and the two rolls were locked together, everything after that would be in sync. That is, until you found that place were the camera battery was running low, which caused the camera to run at a slightly slower speed, which caused the lip-sync to drift. At that point, you would either tuck the sound up a few frames or add a few frames to re-sync the picture and sound. In video, you have none of those problems, especially if you are using a system with built in time code and inner-lock capability between multi-camera set ups. If you do not have this luxury, then make a simple clapboard slate and use it to inner-lock the two cameras by finding the frame where the pop occurs and match it with the other camera's take of the same time. All should match provided you do not turn either camera off and then back on during the take.

Lighting For Cinema-verite'

A discussion on cinema-verite' would not be complete without considering the lighting set up problems. This documentary style of shooting inherently means no concern for lighting. If you are shooting 35MM film that may be okay due  to the extreme latitude of film emulsion to capture an image no matter how bad the lighting is at your location. Unfortunately, video does not have that latitude, so certain precautions must be taken in order to create an acceptably viewable frame.

There are a number of choices that you may want to consider and test to find what will work best for you. I am a strong believer of three point lighting, taught to me by Peter Gibbons, in his sixties at the time and as full of energy as ever. He shot many of the Cinerama pictures in the fifties and early sixties, including "How the West Was Won". This, for me, is the starting place for any lighting set up. Another style is the use of soft lighting through the use of bouncing lights off of umbrellas and white cards. A third style is the use of available lighting. The biggest problem with available lighting is that it seldom is available where you want it, and more often, in the lens, just where you do not want it. The one thing video cameras can not handle without adding 'grain' or video noise is the high contrast ratio in available lighting set ups. If you are going to shoot available light, make sure there is plenty of it in order to bring down that ratio.

Backgrounds cause problems in lighting for video cameras as well as film cameras. When the background has a large window, the camera will adjust the exposure to the brightest object in the frame. This being light flooding in the window, everything else is below or darker, as a result, your actor or subject's face will be in silhouette. Since you always want the focus of your frame to be on the subject, you want that to be the brightest area, not the darkest. Bright walls and windows in the background should be avoided if at all possible. If not, then the actors will have to be lit to a brighter value in order to compensate.

Camera Tricks

White balance and filters are becoming more of a problem for young filmmakers because the equipment manufactures are taking  more control away from the artists. In the nineties, we, who came from 35MM and 16MM film backgrounds to the video age, would often 'trick' the video camera's white balance to create a warm or cool look without using colored filters. This was done by showing the camera a light blue card instead of white. When the electronics corrected the blue out to create white, the result was a warm look to the video that we shot. By showing the camera a warm salmon colored card we were able to get a colder look, if we wanted a moon lit look for example. Today's cameras are starting to have circuits that are doing an on-going white balance that will totally negate that technique as well as using a matt box filter system. We can only hope that they will continue to have a manual override for this feature. Of course, at the same time the editing 'boxes' are becoming more sophisticated with ways of making color corrections in post production.

Sound For Cinema-verite'

In keeping with the style of cinema-verite', sound must be as unobtrusive to the shooting as possible. A boom mic would be very difficult to manage especially if you are shooting multi-  camera set ups. At the close up distances involved, the on-board or camera mounted shotgun mics should provide adequate sound recording. In the case of multi-camera set ups, the two mics, having some separation, should provide excellent stereo sound, a luxury the cinema-verite' filmmakers never had.

Dramatic Storytelling

From a dramatic storytelling point of view, cinema-verite' can be very exciting. The fast paced shooting style lends itself to fast paced storytelling, just right for today's market of short attention span viewers.

As the production cost rose on episodic television programs of the sixties and seventies, networks and producers off set this by moving from half hour programs to one hour programs. This effectively doubled the fees paid by the networks to the production companies for their product. During the eighties and nineties these costs skyrocketed as performers demanded more and more money for their participation. Networks countered with more and longer commercial breaks. It is standard for half hour sitcoms to produce only sixteen to nineteen minutes of entertainment for the twenty-nine and one half minute time slot. Proportionally, the one hour dramas are doing the same thing to pay their stars and rising production costs. The "balloon" can be inflated only so much before it will eventually burst. Hollywood has a way of recycling itself in one form or another. The good news for young filmmakers is that they eventually will come looking for you. You have the answer. Fresh ideas, told in new and interesting ways. At the beginning of the new century, networks put reality programs, reality game shows, and investigative news anchor programs on the air in an effort to bring down the cost of programming. It is only a matter of time before they hit on the genius idea of putting thirty minute dramas from filmmaking competitions on the air. They will be paying far less than the usual production costs, and like *America's Funniest Videos*, they will be airing less than high production value material, paying small cash rewards, and reaping huge profits to cover their executive wastes.

The Future is Now

The timing is right for you to be there, ready to go into action with your thirty minute dramas, shot in *gorilla filmmaking* style. What is most exciting about this coming trend is that you have a ring side seat. All that we have discussed in  the previous chapters and the remaining chapters are geared to help you accomplish such a goal, should you so choose. You are learning the basics for lighting, shooting, directing actors, editing, and recording sound and most important, writing a dramatic story.

This is what being a filmmaker is all about. A 'filmmaker' is not a producer, director, editor or writer, he or she is a person who takes a project from beginning to end in all or most of those capacities. My definition of a filmmaker is that they are storytellers, first. No one would question the genius of either Steven Spielberg or George Lucas' ability to tell a good story, but each man approaches it from a different direction in my opinion.

Steven Spielberg is a director and producer. He is not a filmmaker. George Lucas is a filmmaker. Sometimes he has been a director, and usually a producer and always the writer. But first of all he is a storyteller. Whether it is a story about a small California town on one given night or a galactic tale of biblical proportions, he is a great storyteller and that love of storytelling is what drives him. It is a noble goal for any young filmmaker to have. To dream impossible achievements and watch those achievements come to life. Not because you have unlimited funds and the most advanced equipment, but because you have an idea, a simple camcorder, a willingness to work hard, a dream and a belief that you can see it through. In these pages are the tools to bring those dreams to life with not much more than hard work and some team effort by your classmates that share the same dreams. The future is now and you can do it. If you interview successful people who have lived through countless failures and finally found success, they will all tell you the same thing: "I succeeded because I was not willing to give up, I just kept trying, knowing that eventually, I would succeed". Thomas Edison, the famed inventor of many of our modern marvels, tested over a thousand filaments in trying to create the light bulb. Finally, he tested tungsten and found the success for which he was looking. Over a hundred years later we are still using his invention. People who succeed never give up on their dreams, nor should you.

Class Exercise

Create a two-minute film script to take place completely in the hall of your school. The action begins with two students talking at their lockers and continues to the classroom door. It ends with one student entering the class and the other walking on. This will be shot cinema-verite' style by several teams of students, then critiqued by all students participating in the exercise.

Chapter Twenty-Two

Advanced Writing

Any good feature film begins with a good story. You can have the best acting, the best special effects, the best locales, and the best budget, but if you do not have a good story the audience will not tell their friends to go see the  movie. Without word of mouth, all the hype in Hollywood will not save a lousy picture. A good example of this is *Waterworld*, starring Kevin Costner. Costing over one hundred and forty million dollars to shoot made less that eighty million in the first nine weeks and to date has not turned a profit. *E.T.* cost less than ninety million to shoot and made in the neighborhood of one quarter of a billion in the first nine weeks. Nice neighborhood. In *E.T.* we care very much about the little fellow finding his way home. In *Waterworld*, we don't really care what happens to him or his plant. Any good story begins with a good premise.

☐ New York actor can not get work, dresses up in women's clothing and becomes soap star. *Tootsie*, starring Dustin Hoffman

☐ Photographer with broken leg watches neighbors through his rear window, discovers one has murdered his wife and dismembered her body. *Rear Window*, directed by Alfred Hitchcock.

☐ Imprisoned cannibalistic psychopath is interviewed with hope that he can help capture a crazed serial killer. *The Silence of the Lambs*, written by Thomas Harris. [4 Academy Awards]

A good premise can be verbalized in one or two sentences. Like reading a headline in a newspaper, it is designed to get you to read more.

Developing a Premise

To develop a good premise you need to take inventory of what has already been done. A screenwriter friend once said to me: "What Hollywood wants is something that has never been done, but *proven*." He was the veteran of  countless pitches to the networks with story ideas for series. In the old days, if one network aired a program about a comic book character like *Batman*, the next one put on *The Green Hornet*, if one aired *Bewitched*, another countered with *I Dream of Jeannie*. It never changes, one put on *Survivor* as a game show, the others fall in line with another series like *Fear Factor*. Because the networks and studios are run by people not schooled in storytelling, they do not know a good idea when they see one. They can only guess. They can only copy each other. That is why they are so easily blindsided by student films like *The Blair Witch Project*. So forget imitating ideas that have already been done. If you catch yourself describing your idea as: "Being like this movie, *only...*" Stop right there, you need a better premise.

Where do you come up with that next blockbuster premise? Research. And that starts with reading newspaper headlines, magazine articles, news programs, and conversations with people. You should have your 'radar' always tuned to

detecting a good idea. How many times have you heard some true story that sounded so strange that you or someone else said: "That's so bizarre no one would believe it's true." Truth is stranger than fiction. Frequently, a good premise is a blend of two ideas brought together to form a new premise. Think about those possibilities by considering two premises from two movies that have just come out in your town or city. Now think about the same thing from the news.

Inventing Real Characters

Movies that are successful usually fall into the same mold: *Ordinary* people in *extraordinary* circumstances. Logically speaking then, we can assume that if they are ordinary, they are not super heroes and so they must have flaws  like the rest of us. A formula you have seen dozens of times is that of the lead character having some fear, be it snakes, heights, or small spaces. At sometime during the story he or she must face that fear and overcome it in order to save the day. In *Raiders of the Lost Ark*, Indiana Jones finds the trap door in the desert floor to the lost tomb, looks into the Abbess and remarks: "Why is the floor moving... Snakes, I hate snakes." As soon as we see these thousands of snakes we know that he his going to have to overcome this fear. That drives the story. So our characters drive the plot, not the other way around.

We have all met strange, wonderful people, in our lives. Some are quirky, some eccentric, and some just plain weird. They can be a great place to start designing your characters. Imagine this unique person if they were faced with the premise you are considering, how would they handle it? Frequently, as you create a character based on someone you know, as you develop this imaginary person, the character will move away from your original model until you can hardly see the resemblance. This is part of the process, and should be expected.

Generally speaking, your central character needs to have a fatal flaw. In the *Dirty Harry* series of movies, what is Clint Eastwood's character's fatal flaw? He is a darn good policeman, but he has a problem playing by the political rules. His flaw is, he just keeps getting in trouble with his boss because he hates criminals. "What about the victim's rights?" He can be heard saying. That is a chord that rings true for any audience; many have been victimized by criminals who frequently get off on some technicality. In the case of *Dirty Harry,* the flaw is actually a strength to most audience members. What is a common thread in all of this is to remember that not only should your scenes have conflict, your characters should have conflicts within themselves, bring another layer, another texture to the fabric of your tale.

In *Swordfish,* starring John Travolta, we spend most of the movie believing he is a ruthless criminal bent on making money at any cost. In the end we are led to believe that his deep love for country drives him to defend it against terrorists at any cost. His fatal flaw is his unwillingness to seek justice through legal means. Is he a good guy or a bad guy? It depends on your personal point of view. There is a story that has never been done and yet proven. How can this be? Robin Hood for one.

Crafting a Sophisticated First Act

Time and again, movies that start off slow usually fizzle out by the middle of act two and you are either flipping channels or thinking about slipping into another theatre. They do not have enough steam to get the  story through all three acts. What is missing in these stories is a catalyst. The catalyst is something that happens that gets the story moving. An accident, a phone call with bad news, someone knocks on the door, or maybe an announcement on the TV, something that gets the story in motion.

The second device that needs to happen is to present the *set up*. This is usually accomplished by asking the premise question. Will Marty get back to the future? Will Indiana Jones find the lost Ark before the Germans? Will E.T. finally get home? Will Luke Skywalker save the galaxy and find out what his roots really are?

The third factor that needs to be introduced in act one is the central character's personality. If you think about the people you do not care to spend time with, you will probably realize that part of the problem is that they are boring to be around. If your central character has that same trait, your audience will feel the same way. How do you make them interesting? The friends that you do enjoy being around, why do you enjoy them? Identify those traits that interest you and give them to your characters. If you read or watch famous actors talk about pictures they have enjoyed working on, at some point they all say the same thing: "I wanted to do this part because I liked the character, thought it would be interesting..." Good actors look for fascinating characters to play. Tom Hanks greatly improved his box office draw when he made *Big*, directed by

Penny Marshall. The story of a twelve year old boy who wishes to be big, and wakes the next day as a twelve year old mind in a thirty year old body. A part Hanks played brilliantly thanks to excellent direction and a exceptionally written script. I am sure when Hanks first read the script he said: "Now this is different, I can do this!" Or something to that effect.

Besides being an out of the ordinary character, your central character or protagonist should have a dominant characteristic. This dominant trait is sometimes called the character key or spine. Maybe they are compulsive, as Mel Gibson's character was in *Lethal Weapon*. Perhaps they are crazed such as Bette Midler's  character was in *Drowning Mona*. They might be nervously shy as Norman Bates was in *Psycho*. By giving your protagonist and antagonist another dimension, another layer, you make that person more exciting to your audience. Students often say to me that they could never write a screenplay or that writing is too hard for them to even try. After I ask them about some of their ideas, I see that it is the act of writing that scares them, not the lack of ideas. They are a wealth of fresh, imaginative storylines that Hollywood would be lucky to have. So in this text we must help you see your potential by allowing you to see the process that other writers go through to get that final break-through story. Richard Matheson, the writer of *The Incredible Shrinking Man*, a popular sci-fi film of the fifties, said the idea for that story came to him one day when he put on a hat that was too big. He suddenly thought, what if the hat was not too big, but he was actually shrinking? The germ of a great idea was born. You never know from where that next idea may come, but you can do the same as others have, providing you are always on the lookout for something different to be the springboard of a story that has never been done, but proven.

So crafting a sophisticated first act means getting to know your protagonist and giving that person life through the adding on of layers and textures. And the same is true of the antagonist as well. It means creating the theme question or premise question to keep the audience interested, and introducing a catalyst that gets the story moving. In Tim Burton's 2001 version of *Planet of the Apes*, what is the catalyst that gets the story moving? It is the electromagnetic storm that disrupts the space station's electronics. That catalyst drives the story and creates the theme for several story elements developed throughout the three acts. Once you have begun with these aids, you will find that writing is a joy, an adventure, and something you will look forward to doing.

Act Two Complications

As stated in a previous chapter, audience interest thrives on conflict. Without conflict, there is no drama, so your audience is doing not much more than watching laundry dry in a tumble  dryer. The purpose of act two is to keep the story moving through complications. We already know that we need to introduce the *or-else factor* into our story to keep the drama going, the *ticking time bomb* as Hitchcock once referred to it as being.

In a more sophisticated way than just the or-else factor, we need to have turning points in our story. Events that change the direction and create more complications for our protagonist to overcome. A film well worth studying if you are able to find it at Netflix or library is

Midnight Run, starring Charles Grodin and Robert De Niro, released in 1988. This film is an excellent study of a number of writing elements. One, the way the complications create turning points in act two. Two, the way that a seemingly completely unrelated 'A' and 'B' story are fabricated. Three, the way that both of these unrelated stories dovetail into an exciting climax. You may want to watch it more than once in order to study the structure of the script because the hilarious antics along the way make it impossible to watch without getting involved. It is Robert De Niro at his comic best (Until *Meeting the Parents* years later). I have been told that the dry humor of Charles Grodin on set during shooting is one of the most entertaining work days one could have. You can see that sly, tongue in cheek humor, in the twinkling of his eyes as he works. The year it was released was the same year *Rain Man* swept the Oscars which is the only reason I can think of why this did not win in several categories.

Complications through distinct turning points keep a story interesting for the audience. In *Fatal Attraction,* Michael Douglas' character has a one night fling with Glenn Close's character. Had not Close's character decided that she wanted more than one night, the complications she caused would not have driven the story through its nail biting second and third act. This is another film of the late eighties worth seeking out for examination of script writing.

In a technical sort of way the two turning points necessary to build a strong story are the first turning point, which should be placed at the head of act two and one at the head of act three. This does not exclude placing lots of turns and twist along the way to maintain the audience's attention. *Shattered* (1991), starring Tom Berenger has many twists along the way that successfully mask the <u>real</u> turning point at the beginning of act three. It is so first-rate I will not ruin it by giving it away. Find it, and enjoy it. Then study the structure of how the story unfolds for an excellent teaching exercise.

Without question, act two is the most difficult to write. It must contain the necessary complications, twists, turning point and logical plot devises to maintain your audience interest. At the same time, you must be careful to see that your characters are driving the story, not the other way around. The reason this is important is because if you allow the plot to drive the story you end up fabricating unlikely situations. To be sure, countless low budget movies have been structured this way. These are usually movies that were shot on film and went straight to video release. When you watch these films you find that things suddenly pop up out of nowhere and they are not clever twists, they are quirky plot changes that come out of left field. You know the ones to which I am referring. The ones that make you say to yourself: "She would never do that." Or maybe: "Why did he do that, when this would be more logical?" Well, that answer is, the writer was making his or her characters do odd things in order to facilitate the script needs. I call that *situational writing*, meaning the situation drives the story. *Pulp Fiction* is a perfect example of this type. Avoid this kind of writing and you will have much more success.

Act Three Finale and Resolve

The third act begins with the second turning point. Without this turning point the story will become so predictable that your audience will know the outcome before you can get there. To me, the classic *so you think you know where this is going* twist, was in the original *Rocky*, which won best picture in 1976. The night before the big fight, Rocky tells Adrian that he has nothing. All he wants to do is be able to go the whole fifteen rounds with the heavy weight. She is of course convinced that he will die in the ring. Beat to a pulp. So we, as the audience, know from this scene that he has no chance of winning, so we begin cheering for him to just go the fifteen rounds and come out alive. This is a perfect turning point because he has lost his hope of winning. The focal point has changed to staying in the bout no matter what. When he wins the heavy weight championship at the surprise ending we are thrown off guard because of the third act turning point. Stallone did a skillful job writing this script as his first time out. The rest is history. I had the pleasure of shooting a interview with him one day at a golf course for a documentary on Stephen Verona, the director of Stallone's first movie, *The Lords of Flatbush*. He was gracious and as charming and humble in person as he seems to be on talk shows. He is real. I can not mention the name Stephen Verona without commenting what a pleasure I had working hand in hand with him on his project, *Self Portrait*, which chronicles the making of *The Lords of Flatbush* and his many other endeavors. One of the most talented men, in so many areas, that I have ever had the pleasure of knowing, personally.

You have created a story that you have brought from introducing a premise, added complications and turning points, and now it is time for the big finish. In its most simplistic form, it is time for the bully to get his come-upin's, as they say in Texas. For the rest of you: It is time for the bully to get what's coming to him. How do we do that?

As you might guess by now, there are certain rules for how this should be accomplished. You can ignore these rules and re-invent the wheel if you like, but you will soon find that these rules were created out of the thousands of films that were successful or flopped over the past decades.

☐ The antagonist must be defeated by the protagonist, and no one else. No bolts of lighting at the last minute to save the hero from having to use the gun he promised his dying wife he would never pick up again.

☐ The antagonist needs to be more overpowering than the protagonist, otherwise where is the challenge?

☐ The protagonist needs to come to some change in his or her life or thinking. Getting their faith back in human nature or whatever. This is how the resolve is expressed in dialogue and action. Frequently, it is the protagonist overcoming some great fear.

Inventing a Story

As an exercise in writing a simple five minute script to get you started, let us imagine a situation that could be the start of a screenplay. Since it is important to learn to think, first in outline form, before writing the script, we will begin that way.

You will decide the kind of story you want this to be. A comedy, a drama, a sci-fi, a thriller, or even a western. You decide. *The tale all started because of what happened in class this morning:*

• Adam was late for class. Adam has always been on time. Someone remarked that it was not like him to be tardy. As a matter of fact, he did not seem himself.

We have the start of an intriguing plot line. There can be any number of reasons why he was late. If a comedy, we might see a flashback to how this day got started. If a drama, interest can be generated to find out what happened that was so awful that he refuses to discuss it with his friends. If a sci-fi, maybe that is not really Adam, after all we just said he was not himself. Perhaps he is really someone else or *something* else.

What is our premise?

Adam is acting unusual.

Why is he acting that way, and why was he late?

Write down several reasons why this could be. Pick the one you like the best. Now think about a secondary character. Perhaps this character relates to the reason he was late. Let us make it a girlfriend, Beth.

What is going on between Adam and Beth?

Well, we know that it must have conflict, so what is their conflict?

Does one of them want to break up? If so, why? Write down several possibilities. Another guy, another girl, an illness one does not want the other to know about. One is moving away or has to quit school for some reason.

Now think about an antagonist. What are the possibilities based on your previous choices from the list above.

The other guy is jealous? The other girl is crazy? (Or vice-versa)

Maybe the antagonist is a teacher that has it in for Adam. If so why? Does the teacher hate Adam's father because of a bad business deal or lost love from when they were in this same school, years earlier?

Can you believe how easy this is? We have not even begun to scratch the surface for good plot ideas. As you can already see the characters are writing this story, not the plot. The plot is developing *because* of the characters.

What else do we know about what is going on with Adam? Someone will have to find out by asking some probing questions of Adam after class.

Charlie would be a good one for that job. They have been friends since grade school. Or maybe his sister, Dawn. Maybe both.

As you create more layers of interest for your audience, you should be aware of one very important obligation and responsibility you now have. You must have a payoff for the audience that is worthy of the investment of time that they have made in your story. A weak payoff after a big or long build up will frustrate your audience. In short they feel cheated.

Perhaps you may have noticed that our character names begin with the first letters in the alphabet. They also alternate between male and female. This is to show that you need not waste a lot of time thinking up clever names for your characters at this point. They can all be changed, once you have an idea that works. Any distraction at this stage slows or even stops the mental flow of ideas. That is all you want right now, ideas.

Let us take inventory of what we have at this point. Adam was late, will not talk about it and we do not know why. We have not introduced the *or else factor*.

What would you like for an or else factor?

Should we say that it is the fact that he is not talking? Maybe he can't. Perhaps if he tells, the *or else* kicks in.

That brings us to the catalyst, the event that kicks the story into gear. What is a likely catalyst, based on the choices of story type and characters that you have made so far?

Adam has a conversation with a stranger after class?

He gets a call on his cell phone and turns ashen white with fear?

He drops a letter out of his pocket and seems desperate to retrieve it before someone notices it?

And now we need some more complications for him to face. These complications will be examples of the or else factor, until they create the first turning point. They will intensify the choices you have already made. It is important to write down each idea you have had in case one leads to another. If you use several, be sure that the weaker ones are used first so that your story builds.

Remember: Ordinary people in *extraordinary circumstances.*

Like the branch of a tree that keeps branching off, the permutations of different possibilities just keep growing for unique directions this story could go so I can no longer make suggestions on where to take this idea. But by now the ideas you are having that are unique to your story are flowing. You can take it from here and create an interesting five minute screenplay. That should be about five pages at one minute each. In order to keep it to five pages you must be thrifty with your dialogue. Do not waste screen time rambling or restating the theme. Get to the point of each scene and then get out. Have fun. Who knows, maybe your ideas may lead to a story that becomes a film I will get to see someday.

Class Exercise

Present your script to the class.

Chapter Twenty-Three

Advanced Visual Dialogue

In filmmaking, lighting is one of the most important elements and yet it is the most often overlooked aspect of the production for the beginner filmmaker. More important than  reading this chapter is to study the work of many filmmakers of the past to see what has been done by the professionals. One of the best ways of doing this is to watch old movies on television with the sound off so that you will not be distracted by the storyline. Pick a variety to watch, from black and whites to epics, from simple stories to horror films, you should study as many styles as possible to get a range of ideas on how to light sets, actors and locations. As you see how others have done it, you will understand these pages much more clearly, and you will find that certain aspects of lighting make more sense to you as you practice the craft of dramatic lighting.

Parts of Visual Speech

As you learned in a previous chapter, the key light is always placed near the camera, pointing at the subject. This casts a strong shadow behind the subject, usually on the wall and floor. When placing this light as a beginner there is a tendency to focus your attention on the shadow and wonder how to get rid of it, as it seems so noticeable. As a test, I examined a number of blockbuster films with only that potential problem on my mind. As I expected, all had key light shadows on the walls and floors behind the actors. The point is, you as the audience, never notice those shadows. So forget about it. If you can not live with the shadows, then place a smaller fill light aimed at the wall to wash out the shadow. You will see that is far less attractive than allowing the shadows to be there. As you learned before, the key light is close to the camera, pointing toward the subject. On the opposite side of the camera, forty-five degrees off axis, you place the fill light whose intensity is about one half to one third of the key light's intensity. There is a small, uneducated, group of cinematographers who actually think that you are suppose to place the key light at the forty-five degree angle and place the fill light next to the camera. This places a hard shadow on the face of the actor on the side opposite the key light. So from the nose on across the side of the cheek, the face becomes noticeably darker. You just try to convince a highly paid actor that you are going to light them that way and see how long you last as the cinematographer or D.P. On the first few episodes of *CSI:Crime Scene Investigators* on CBS, starring William Petersen, the D.P. was lighting all the actors that way. It was so annoying that I was sure that I would have to give up watching what I thought was a great program. Several episodes into the season, they stopped lighting with that style. Here's my guess, the number of shows they had in the 'can' before it first aired was just about the same number of shows that had this awful style. In other words, they fired the D.P. or viewers complained so much they were forced to re-educate the him. So the style changed as soon as they had feedback it was not working for the audience. Word to the wise: Don't try to reinvent the wheel.

Painting With Light

You may have noticed that throughout the text, there has been no mention of F/stop, foot candles, emulsion speeds or light meters. During the years that I shot 35MM and 16MM films I was seldom without both my light meter and my cinematographer's manual. When I shot Betacam SP video I found more and more that I just never used either. I used my trusted expensive Sony portable monitor fed from the camera and lit the set that way. After years of lighting with 5K's, 2K's, 1K's, Mickey Moles and soft lights, I found that I already knew what the light was going to do and how much I needed for a given situation. If you are lighting primarily for video, you may want to own a light meter to light with it. If not, you will discover that you can train your eye to paint the light by turning the camera on and feeding a good, high quality Sony monitor to get a very good idea of what you are getting on your media storage device. There are also some excellent books on the subject of F/stop, foot candles, emulsion speeds and light meters if you would like to expand your working knowledge of the subject.

Picking The Right Light

As discussed in a previous chapter, there is a problem with some of the smallest lights having too much light intensity. In most average size rooms with white walls a 1K can blast the room so that there is no mottling on the subject to speak of. The easy answer to that problem is lower wattage. Another is, use a dimmer, but that changes the color temperature, which is a whole new subject we will cover later. When you can not lower the wattage for some reason, then you have a number of options.

There is a law in physics called the inverse square law which you may be aware of, if not, briefly it works like this: If you place a light, let's say a candle, one foot from a white card. All of the light hitting the card creates the light of one foot candle. If you place the same candle two feet from the card, the same amount of light now lights four square feet. [See Illustration] Your light is deluded, as it were, so that the same amount of light must cover four square feet instead of one, so the card is now reflecting only one fourth the light, and therefore the inverse square law. What this means to you, is if you move the light stand back from your subject, you will see the light level drop. So one way of reducing the light on your subject is to simply back the light away from the subject, while watching the monitor (Or light meter) until the level you want is achieved.

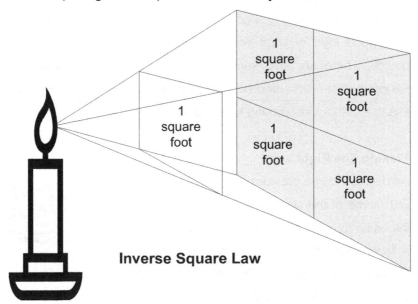

Inverse Square Law

The second way of reducing a light is to partially block off the light emitted from the light fixture with what is called a scrim. This is a screen wire mesh frame that comes with most lighting kits to lower the light level, mechanically. It fits directly on the light itself and soon becomes quite hot. If the light is very bright, you may need to add several scrims. Normally, if you find this is the case too often, you are using lights that are too bright.

The third way of reducing the light level on the subject is to use a Cukaloris, often called a "cookie" in the trade. You can make a

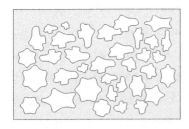

cookie out of foam core to be placed a foot or two from the light on a separate stand. If you place a cookie too close to the light fixture, you will soon see smoke, and if you stand there long enough without doing

something about the problem, you will see fire. If that happens, you have burned your cookie! And maybe the set. The cookie has randomly cut holes all over the face of the card. For a similar effect, if you wanted the light to look like it was coming through the branches of a tree you might place a small, thickly leaved branch a couple of feet from the light. The light hitting the subject has been partially blocked by some leaves, creating a pattern on the subject. As an experiment in class, take such a branch and place it between the light and your test subject. You will notice an important fact you should remember for future reference. As you move the branch closer to the subject, you will discover that the edges of the shadows on the subject become very sharp, well defined lines or edges of the leaves. As you move the branch closer to the light and farther from the subject, you will see that the shadows are more muted. You can no longer see the edges of any one leaf. You will also notice that on the subject, the patterns of light and dark have blended so that there is no hard light next to a hard shadow. This is another way to reduce light without creating hard shadows.

The next item in the gaffer's bag of tricks is the flag. The flag is a metal frame in a variety of sizes, which is covered with black cloth. And as you have already guessed, its shape is how it got its name. The purpose of a flag is very much like the use of a barn door on a light. It blocks off all of the light in one area or in one direction. Flags are often used to shade a part of a wall or ceiling or floor in the background. Flags are expensive on several levels. One, they are expensive to buy and each one requires its own stand (Also expensive to buy) so that it can be placed just where you want it. Two, after placing a couple of flags in one area, you will discover that the stands take up a lot of floor space in front of the light. Three, they take a lot of set time to set up and strike. They are easily damaged so you can not just throw them around. With all of those negatives, it is difficult to justify using them at all. You have only to see what beautiful effects can be achieved to know why they are so important on big budget movies.

Soft Lights

Another important lighting effect is the use of soft lights. There are a number of ways to create a soft light, which is a stage light that has been bounced off of a reflective surface to defuse the light from creating hard shadows. An easy way of thinking about soft lights is to say they are like the light from a fluorescence tube. One of the most popular and often used soft lights is an umbrella attached to a 1K Lowel light. Lowel also makes an excellent 2K soft light that has its own special 'chicken coop'. Another way to create a soft light is to make one from foam core or plywood. The name chicken coop came from the shape used in the design of light. The light is aimed up at the gabled end 'roof' of the coop so that the light bounced off the two apposing white surfaces and then down on to the set.

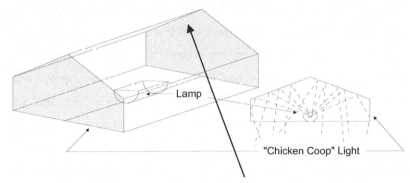

Leave a small opening along the top for heat to escape.

D.P.s will sometimes use this kind of soft light overhead to create a softer version of an overhead key light. On film the effect is quite lovely.

If you wanted to create a scene that takes place at a pool table, you might use this kind of a light instead of using hard lights that are normally over a pool table, which make it difficult to remove unwanted shadows on the actors. Soft lights are a style of lighting that you should consider before using them without forethought.

Color Temperature

In film, the cinematographer or D.P. is concerned with color temperature. What is color temperature? The various sources of light in our world do not emit the same tint of light.

Daylight is bluish and tungsten or light bulb light is yellowish. The human brain receives this visual information from the eye and white balances it so that we see both as white. Color film can not do this, so they are manufactured to balance the quality of a particular light source. These different sources are measured in *Kelvin degrees*. Tungsten film is balanced for 3200 degrees Kelvin. Daylight film is balanced for 6000 degrees Kelvin, which is the color temperature of an overcast day. This is very important if you are shooting on film because you must choose the right type of film and use the right filter. The reason is, if you are using tungsten film indoors and you have window light coming in, it will be 6000 degrees Kelvin and therefore look bluish. You will either have to filter the window with filter material to balance it to 3200 degrees Kelvin or filter the camera. If you tried to use a Lowel light outdoors, which is balanced at 3200 degrees Kelvin, it would throw a warm light on the subject. This would require placing a blue gel on the light to filter it to 6000 degrees Kelvin. Video cameras have a electronic white balance to do a lot of this for you. You still cannot mix the two light sources without seeing the effect of the mix if you turn on the light after white balancing for exterior use.

In film, using a dimmer causes the color temperature to drop below the 3200-Kelvin level the lights normally put out. As the dimmer lowers the light level it will also cause the light to appear more warm or reddish. You can use this effect to your advantage if you want to create a fireplace or campfire effect. I watched the late John Alcott use this technique on the original *Beastmaster* (1984) feature film for our many interior scenes where the light source was supposed to be from torches and campfires. [Author's note: My credit on that film was Assistant Art Director] In video, the use of a dimmer is less of a problem because you only have to re-white balance to correct for the lower wattage of the dimmer. If you are going to use a dimmer in video to bring the wattage down, keep in mind what that does to the color temperature by checking your set up monitor.

Complicated Lighting Techniques

In film, if you want a portion of the frame to go dark, you simply remove the light from hitting that part of the set through the use of flags and scrims. A technique used very well by Dean Cundey in John Carpenter's *Halloween*. In  video, you begin to pick up grain or video noise if there is a lack of light. To correct this short coming of using video you need to have some degree of light on all of the set and hope to bring it down in post by lowering the 'pedestal'. A  trick taught to me when I was still doing film production was to always have a blue light somewhere on the set. Very small, and not even noticeable to the naked eye, but enough to expose the blue layer of the film negative to reduce the grain. By the same token, using a dark blue gel on what little light you allow in that dark part of the set, should help to reduce the noise and still appear very dark. I think not allowing the absence of light in the frame is a part of videography that has not been explored enough. We have all seen the overpowering noise problem from video shot on the streets at night with only street lights for illumination in reality programs (*Cops*), so it is well established to not allow grain or noise to flood the video frame in professional productions. Not breaking this rule prevents creating wonderful lighting such as *Halloween* or the lighting of the forties and early fifties black and white films. Exploring the use of 50 watt halogen lights to replace 1K Lowel lights is an important step in you developing a style that will permit you to have your video productions rival film in its look. Of course there are other things you can do to the camera to enhance this effect, such as a number one diffusion filter over the lens.

Setting the Mood

As a student or just starting out in the business in video lighting and camera work it is difficult to do creative lighting set ups. The beauty of class situations is having the time to do some experimenting with mood lighting. Generally speaking, the filmmaker will use dark illumination to set a somber, tragic mood,  bright illumination to establish a happy, light atmosphere and a variation of the two extremes to fit a variety of moods in between. If all you know how to do is turn on the lights, all you will be able to create is a light, happy mood. So it is important that you learn how to create  dark illumination lighting to express a somber mood to your audience.

Until now we have discussed placing the key light close to the camera to create three point lighting, now it is time to move the key light. Imagine a completely dark room for this experiment we are about to consider. The reason you place the key light close to the camera is to avoid unwanted shadows on the actor's face from their nose and eyebrows. Now imagine a strong overhead key light which will create hard shadows on the face, making the eye sockets look like deep pools of black. By placing a much lower intensity fill light opposite the key you can soften this effect so that some detail is seen in the eyes. So one of the first things we discover doing this is that there is a greater difference between the intensity of the key light and the fill light. If glamour lighting is a three to two ratio between the key and fill, then this kind of lighting is four to one or greater. Sometimes when lighting with a key light pointing down from a high angle, the fill light need be nothing more than a bounce card of foam core. This can be true of glamour lighting as well as mood lighting.

Collecting a Bag of Tricks

As you develop your understanding of lighting you will want to collect an assortment of things that work for you. Foam core in several sizes, some reflective card that bounces less light than foam core, foam core with aluminum foil glued to it, colored  cards for tricking the white balance, cukaloris of several shapes and degrees of light passing, and of course plenty of gels in various colors. As you figure out what works best for you, you will create a package of this gear. You will learn to reduce this to a manageable size by doing things like having one side of the foam core white, the other silver from the foil. You want the light balancing cards as small as possible, with one color on one side and another color glued to the back. The same for your lighting package, use lights as small as possible. You might even use low voltage lights that run on twelve volts (Via transformer) so that you can also run them off of car batteries. The beauty of this light weight package is your ability to get everything in the trunk of your car or back of your school van.

Working with a Budget

You can easily spend thousands of dollars on light packages with stands, lights of all sizes, flags, scrims, filters, gels, cukaloris of various designs, black out fabrics, silks (Large frames with silk fabric stretched on them to shade a  scene in the sun), and four by eight sheets of foam core. If you do have such a package you will also need a semi-trailer to haul it in. Until that time you will want to learn how to have the look all of these things can give you without the expense. That is what is so exciting about the video camcorder, much of these elements of lighting can be achieved in the camera through its electronics. What you still need is a source for smaller lights. Any Ace hardware store, or Home Depot carries these fifty watt halogen lights in a flood or semi-spot lamp. Through special order you can locate a more narrow spot to put light into a smaller portion of the frame. Through the use of some simple dimmer, you can dial the light level down to just the right amount. That leaves only the problem of the fixture itself, finding several to make up a small lighting package so that you can create mood lighting.

Night Exteriors

The final area that needs special direction is the task of lighting exterior night scenes. Exterior night requires light blue gels on the light fixture. The reason for this is as much tradition as it is a requirement. In films we have seen, the night scenes all have a bluish tint to them, the tradition being that Hollywood has always portrayed moon light as being slightly blue. Actually it is more white than  blue but since our brains at night color correct the warm incandescent light bulb as white, our brain further color corrects the whiter moon light over into the blue range. So rule number one is to use a blue gel on the lights that represent the ambient moon light. You can use your color corrector cards to trick the camera's white balance into thinking the orange mercury vapor street lights are blue gelled lights. Testing of your results long before the shooting date.

Getting the Right Perspective

The next problem to solve is the lack of depth of perspective due to light falling off into dark. In other words, without a number of lights deep in the background your  frame will just look like a dark hole or abbess. Hollywood over the decades has had water trucks to wet the streets so that the light would reflect off of the pavement to show that depth and perspective. As film stocks continue to improve, they are doing that less, thanks to pumping more light into the frame through faster emulsions. What you, as a filmmaker on a budget, should do, is to place your lights at various places in the background to show that depth. An example of this would be the scene in *Back to the Future* (Part I), in the shopping mall parking lot, where Marty first time travels in the DeLorean. The parking lot lights gives us that depth because we can see them in the distance, in neat rows and columns. Public places like shopping malls are great places to shoot at night for that very reason, most of your mood lighting has been taken care of for you. So rule number two is to light the background so that the audience has a feeling of depth. If you do not, you might as well shoot them in front of a black curtain, because to the audience, that is what it will look like you did.

Separation

The next lighting problem to solve in night exteriors is to separate the actor from the background. This means bringing the light level in the foreground up so that the subject looks lighter than the background. If you want the subject to appear in an ominous way from the shadows, you merely have to place a strong  overhead light that does not light the dark walls the actor is standing against, as the actor moves into the over head light he will materialize from the shadows. So rule number three is to light the subject in the foreground with a higher value than the background.

Asking the Right Questions

Now that you understand how the scene should be lit, you need to start over with some specific questions that you will want to ask yourself as you survey the potential location with the director. What is the light  motivation for the scene? Is it a campfire in the middle of nowhere? Is it a city street with street lights and business signs all around? Is it a single porch light somewhere in the distance with moon light as one other source of  motivation? You may well be bringing much more light to the scene through your use of your own artificial lights, but never-the-less, you will be making each light you add look like it is part of the original source, be it street  light, moon light, or campfire light. Finding what your light motivation is before you start will help you decide how much and what you want that light source to be. Generally speaking, if you can learn to light exterior night scenes in believable ways, you can light anything. It probably is the most fun to light as well.

Class Exercise

Videotape any night scene from a popular television series where a night scene has been lit by a professional film crew. Draw a lighting plan that you feel best represents where the lights were placed to achieve this look. Each student should present and explain his or her diagram of the expected lighting plan.

Chapter Twenty-Four

Planning the Shoot

Directors come in all favors to be sure, and each like to work in a different way. Complicated features like *Star Wars* rely heavily on storyboards to plan their shooting schedule and plotting the action. Alfred Hitchcock was famous  for his "book" with some of the most beautiful and intricate storyboards ever made. Steven Spielberg favors exact scaled models to use his 'viewing glass' for planning exact shots and shooting angles. Few directors can look at a floor plan of the set or location and visualize how to plan the action and blocking. Some can only work by 'walking the set'. Lucille Ball was known to insist that the stage be off limits to everyone for an hour or so as she sat quietly in an audience seat and visualized her performance of her sit-com in front of the live audience.

The common factor is that all of these people do one thing. They spend time planning the shoot before the other team members arrive. They get a sense of where the action should take place and how best to block that action. A famous director once said: "Keep the actors moving or the camera moving." To that I might add: "If you do not want the audience to start moving...(out)" Another one said you should keep one actor standing. These are not hard rules, just things to think about.

Blocking the Action

How do you block actors? One possible  starting point to answer that question is to find a copy of *Rope* by Alfred Hitchcock. This was a unique experiment in filmmaking. Film rolls in 35MM cameras last for slightly over ten minutes. The longest possible take is therefore about ten minutes. Hitchcock reasoned, what if you blocked the action, almost as a stage play into continuous scenes lasting ten minutes? The scenes would end with an actor in a dark suit walking up to the camera and blacking out the frame. The next take would begin with the same actor starting out against the camera lens and walking away. The story takes place in a New York apartment so the set was an elaborate mechanical set with moving walls to facilitate the huge camera dolly used in the fifties. With a seven to ten minute take in progress, the actors could not make any mistakes since there was no option to cutting away to clean up the flubbed line of dialogue. One mistake and they all start over.

In short, it was a nightmare, never to be tried again. What is important is it is a living testimony to the genius of Hitchcock, and a teaching tool for you. Get a copy of the film and turn the sound off and watch the blocking. You will learn more about how to move actors to and away from the camera for emphasis and visual focus than you could ever learn in a book. A second source for blocking study is to watch a soap opera. These daytime dramas have a standard number of working sets that seldom change and require constant use in diverse ways. They also have little time to spend working out blocking. Outside of Broadway, soap actors and directors work harder than any other group. I know, having spent some time learning the craft in departments on *Days of Our Lives*.

Breaking Down the Shots

There are three main areas to concern yourself with in any scene blocking. The first is the position of the camera or foreground. The second is the plane at which the actor is located. The third is the background.

One may determine the other's position. If you have a strong light coming in a window that you want to avoid, then that will determine either the position of the actor, the camera, or both. There are always limitations so you want to begin by working around the things that you can not change.

Once you have established the directions that are useable, the next consideration should be to think about the fact that you need a wide shot and two close ups. What problems will that cause? One close up may be looking right into that window. You may need to move the furniture about.

Two Examples of strong window light flooding the 'set'

After the 'traffic' areas have been decided, you next want to think about what is important in the scene. This comes from examining the dialogue. What is important for you to get across to the audience? Is it one key word or phrase? Is it a story point they could easily miss? Is it a facial reaction by one of the actors?

Blocking Techniques

A classic standby for both Hitchcock in *Rope* and the daily soaps is the use of placing one actor close to the camera, facing the camera, as the other actor in the distance looks at the back of the actor's head. The actor in the distance can not see the reaction on the actor's face close to the camera but the audience can, close up and personal. So we, as the audience, get certain visual information the other actor does not. This is one way to see what an actor is thinking without the use of that annoying  voice over of the actor's thoughts. This technique also allows using one angle for both the wide shot and the close up at the same time. (Racking focus from one to the other is how you change the audience's attention from one to the other as needed.) This saves editing more cuts into the scene. One actor can be in close up while we still see the rest of the set in wide shot. By moving the other actor up to the first, we have a two shot without cutting. Or by allowing the first actor to walk away from camera, it becomes a wide shot for the two actors. So by using stage performance style blocking you can make one camera angle serve more than one camera position which can save set up and lighting time if you are under a time budget problem.

Making it Natural

Most situations in scenes are of people in natural environments doing what people do like eating, sitting, walking, working in the garden, working on a bike or car, sitting at a computer, or soaking in a tub. As an example of that, I have a visual image of a great scene in a western movie I have since forgotten (It probably was *McCabe & Mrs. Miller* Directed  by R. Altman) of a cowboy with his hat on, smoking a cigar, while soaking in a tub covering vital parts with soap suds and enjoying a good sipping whiskey. If I can remember a scene from a movie over forty years old it must have had a dynamic impact on me. Why did I remember it? Because the director took the time to show the audience how much just getting to take a bath was in those frontier days. We have all seen movies where some guy was in a tub scrubbing down with soap, big deal. Can you remember what movie and who? No impact.

Finding the Subtext

So you want to use the location and situation to express more to your audience than the script shows. That comes from looking between the lines or as my production designer friend Bill Strom says, look for the  subtext of the script and the characters in the story. What is their background, motivation, needs and drives?

Finding the Spine of the Scene

Once you have broken down the scene to what is important to show the audience, you are ready to look at how you want the scene to start and where you want it to stop. These two points have importance when it comes to transitions from the previous scene to the next. Most movies seem to care little about transitions from one scene to the next. They just cut them and stick one on to the next. As mentioned before, Danny De Vito's direction of *Hoffa* had brilliant transitions from one scene to the next. They were well thought out and well planned long before the scenes were shot. *Never* miss a film directed by Mr. De Vito.

Look for Simplicity

By knowing where to start and where to stop, you then know what has to be done to fill in the blanks. If you have for example, an actor starting a scene by lighting a cigar at his fancy desk and ending the scene with him crushing the cigar in an ash tray on the window sill looking out over the city, then you know we have to get from one point to the next in some logical manner. If the scene includes him being interrupted by his secretary entering with important news, then you want to choreograph all of this action in a natural way and at the right timing. You might, for example, have a location that allows you to start close on the desk and actor as the cigar is lit, pan as the actor gets up and walks away from camera to a wider shot of the expensive office, stop as the secretary enters with the note or dialogue, continue panning as she leaves and follow the actor as he considers the information and walks passed the camera to the window. The camera has made a slow sweep of the room in a two hundred and seventy degree arc and ended in another medium shot of the ash tray at the window. One simple blocking move with no other camera set ups needed for this particular set of action needs. So planning the wide shot or cover shot first allows you to see just where the scene will take you.

Discovering What is Key

Very scene is a piece of a larger puzzle that you are creating for you audience. It can be a feature length story, a documentary, or a commercial or video presentation. They all require the same thing, focus on what is important for that moment.

Since the above list all have a scene of some type in them, we can keep our interest on that level in gaining understanding how to master plan the scene. If every scene, like the whole story, has a beginning, middle and an end, then we want each scene to make a point or build to some climax within itself. If that point is made at the beginning of the scene we hardly need go further. So each scene plays a part in telling our story. It may be some information about the character, or the plotline, or the background that brought the story about. If it does not bring this to the total picture why is it in the film? As filler? We do not need fillers. We need substance. Substance comes from dialogue and situations that move the story along in a logical, clear way that the audience call follow. Each scene is either a set up, or a payoff of the story structure. What is in between those two? Fluff? Time killers? Both are audience killers, so leave them out. That hard and cold fact of life will make you realize that each scene is vital to the story or it would not be there. And therefore you need to learn to treat each scene with the respect that it deserves by planning it carefully and making sure that you are not 'sanding off the edges' of this puzzle piece to make it fit with the rest. Remember this: Audiences are able to make a bigger jump than you think so avoid wasting time telling them something that is not important to moving the story along. "But I love this scene, even if it does not fit." Yeah? Put in another film for insomniacs that need a sleep aid.

Developing the Original

As you break down a scene and look for what is key to telling the story, you want to study the script for what is there, what is implied, what is in between the lines, what is hidden from the other characters for now, what needs to be expressed to the audience in a verbal and visual way, and what can be used as a device to set up the next chain of events in the story. One example might be for the character to pocket something without the other character seeing it, something that has importance later on. That might not have been in the script but makes perfect sense as you break down the scene. Look for *pieces of business*, as it is called, that help tell the story.

We have only scratched the surface on all the tricks and gimmicks that are used to 'sell' a scene to the audience. As you have read many times by now in this text, your best teacher are the films that you watch, not once but over and over. You need not spend a lot of money to see the latest blockbuster, the old movies on TV offer a wealth of insight and knowledge for you to take at your own speed. Good writers read other writer's work.

The same goes for filmmakers.

Chapter Twenty-Five

Working with Actors

As a young director wannabe, I took more than a few acting classes in an effort to learn what actors go through and how to communicate with them in a way that would be easy for them to understand. Acting is not at all easy, in fact, film acting is one of the  hardest types of acting because of its special requirements. One of my teachers who was working with several of us, including Judge Reinhold, and a number of others who have become well known, was asked by me what to do when an actor just can not seem to give you what you want? How do you work with them to get a performance? His answer was: "You don't. You fire them and get someone else." Yikes! That was not the answer I was expecting. It turned out to be pretty good advise.

The problem of Overacting

As a young director working with inexperienced actors, one of the most common problems that you will face is overacting. Almost all actors when they first get started make that mistake. Everything that comes out of their mouth sounds phony or like they are reading the line badly. You will not hear the overacting as you first begin to work with them, but eventually you will develop an ear for what sounds natural.

You can not exactly go around firing student actors for not giving the performance for which you were hoping, as my instructor suggested. Try to remember that you are learning as well, and your directing may well be worse than their acting. How to we fix that?

One of the best illustrations that explains what is happening with the young or inexperienced actor is the following: The acting assignment is to play a drunk in a public situation. The beginning actor will play drunk for all that it is worth. Everything will be exaggerated. The point that an inexperienced actor is missing is what happens to a person who has had several drinks. An experienced actor will dissect the part for what is going on beneath the surface. A drunk does not know that anything has changed. They think they are being normal. They are not aware that they are moving more slowly, that their speech is impaired, or that they are having trouble keeping their balance. So in essence, what the experienced actor is doing is playing a drunk *trying* to act sober. Now instead of playing the part over the top, they simply play the person who is moving more slowly, finding it hard to remember the right words they want to use, constantly readjusting their balance and because they are reacting more slowly, find that each readjustment overcompensates for the last. They are a tower of weaving adjustments. If they knock something off the table they reach to stop it from falling long after it has hit the floor. These are the subtleties that make a part like that work. The most difficult aspect of acting for the beginner actor is to understand how to make it seem normal, effortless, and unforced. Your job is to help them find that place. Some good advice given to me was from a close friend, Perry King, an actor of motion pictures and television series. He said of working with beginning actors, tell them that no matter what, don't *act*.

Easy Does It

Another problem that beginners have is to either rush through a scene or freeze up with nothing at all. You have only to watch someone like Anthony Hopkins' work in *Silence of the Lambs*, *Magic*, or one of his other exceptional performances to see how he paces himself in a scene. If a line of dialogue is delivered to him and he does not answer back immediately, as you watch him in that moment, you do not feel that he is trying to think of his next line, you know that as the character, he is considering his reply. There is a difference. He is controlling the timing of the scene with the presence that he commands as an actor. He plays a scene in a style that is called: *playing it under*. That is always more interesting than playing it *over* the top. Clint Eastwood has a similar approach. In his case, there is a controlled anger just under the surface, ready to boil over at any moment. Without saying a word we sense that anger. What is it that they are doing? They are under-acting. There is a line of distinction between under-acting and being just plain boring. The difference is energy. Actors often hear the phrase: "This time with a little more energy." That does not mean more force in their voice, or more excited. It means act like it is important and real, not something that is being read from a page. Good directors usually give little direction, and yet know exactly how to communicate with their actors in a way that the actor will understand. If you want to be a good director, you must put in the time to work with your actors in rehearsals and improvisations that teach you both how to communicate with each other.

Keeping the Actors Informed

Actors are *putting it out there* as they say, and taking chances as they play a part. For that reason and others they deserve to be kept informed about what is expected of them and what all is taking place in this scene and the one leading up to this scene. Take the time to explain what you want and how you see the scene should be played. That will help them prepare and they will appreciate your input in giving them direction. Maybe they are stumped about how to play the scene. If you talk it over with them and they suggest a different approach, suggest that you rehearse it their way and see if it works. If does not, at least they will have had a test drive down an unknown road, which will give them more confidence to try another road-namely the one you want. You can not inform the actors if you do not know the direction you are taking them so it is important that you spend time beforehand dealing with the script so that you know the subject matter. If you are not prepared, how do you tell them what you want? If you don't know what you want, why are you directing others?

An excellent class exercise would be to take a short scene from a popular movie, play it in class and then break up into a few groups and shoot the scene for yourselves.

The rules include:

☐ You may only watch the scene one time before working out your version.

☐ The scene should not be longer than two minutes in length.

☐ The groups should include no more than two actors, one director, one person lighting and doing the camera work.

☐ You may light one set and use it for all groups if you like.

☐ You may shoot the scene only once, however you may

rehearse the scene as many times as you like away from the "set".

☐ The instructor or teacher will have to transcribe the necessary dialogue so that students do not become too familiar with the movie version of the material.

One way of doing this is to decide at one class meeting which scene will be transcribed so that the instructor can have the printed scene ready for the next meeting.

Notes:

Chapter Twenty-Six

Preparing For The Real Marketplace

The opening lines in chapter eighteen bare repeating:

- People hardly find out you are interested video production before they are calling you to videotape their weddings, bar mltzvahs, anniversaries and maybe a local commercial or promotional video for a relative's company. Occasionally they may actually pay you for the services you render. Only you can decide how much of this social abuse you want to endure before putting your foot down and start charging a scheduled fee for your services.

Once you cross that line into printing business cards, stationery, and getting a business phone you will find that you are running a business with all of its ups and downs, including proper payments to local, state, and federal tax agencies. All of these items are expenses that you <u>will</u> be paying out, so keep that in mind when your friends, relatives, and strangers ask you to work for less. As you make the transition from student to filmmaker you can allow yourself to be slightly abused business wise. They get a product from a talented person for far less than the commercial rate, and you get some hands on experience in situations unlike school and more like the real world. It will also help you purchase equipment along the way that you will be using as you create your own business. I know of no one in the industry that does not do *something* on the side in a entrepreneurial way. Eventually so will you, only because word gets around and they *will* come calling sooner or later.

Special Events

One of the first kinds of projects you will find yourself involved in are the family events recording. As listed above they include the wedding, bar mitzvah, anniversary, and maybe a baptismal. These projects have a natural focus on the event, not you, so like a still photographer, you want to blend into the woodwork and be as little noticed as possible, which means shooting available light as much as possible. If the event includes a sit down dinner, then there is usually a time that you can move about the crowd to record interviews with the guests about the host(s). If it is a wedding, then be sure to get a comment from all of their friends. Later the couple will enjoy watching these interviews, especially if you shoot and edit it professionally with background music and titles. Beginners all make the same mistake. They make it far too long. Like *60 Minutes*, you must learn to cut the interviews very short. As you shoot, think about how it will be edited. For example, you might edit the interviews into one string, all answering the same question. "What did you think of her dress?"

"Did you think he looked nervous?" By asking each friend a few quick questions that create an open to funny answers, you will get a string of silly answers that the couple will have fun watching tagged together. You start each section with a black screen and title that might read: "Kathy's Dress"

You cut out your voice of the question, leaving only their answers. This theme or one similar that you create will have a winning appeal to your clients because consumers do not think of videotaped weddings as being edited in a *60 Minutes* style and pace. But of course, that is why you charge what you do and why you *can* charge what you do. You *are* a professional. Whenever possible, you want a locked down wide shot camera on a tripod and a second camera for closer shots that you handle yourself. This will allow you editing options.

The following list suggest the kinds of shots you want to remember to get for whatever event it may be. These cutaways allow you some editing latitude if you have equipment or location sound problems.

☐ Audience reaction shots

☐ Close ups of the flowers, Bibles or scripture scrolls, cards, stain glass windows.

☐ People being seated.

☐ All of the people taking an active part in the ceremony such as the Cantor, musician(s), minister, Rabbi, priest, soloist.

☐ Establishing shot of the building where the event takes place.

☐ Vehicles, if they are important to the event.

☐ Cake, gifts, decorations, food, open bar.

This is some inside information to keep to yourself:

When people spend a lot of money on an event, they want it recorded for a lot of reasons including how much they spent. If you do not shoot every aspect of the examples of that expense, they will be somewhat disappointed. Conversely, if you make that expenditure look like even more was spent, they will think you are a genius young filmmaker and they will promote you to their friends. You see, it is an embarrassing thing for them to tell you to be sure and shoot how much they spent, so they probably will not be comfortable telling you that. You should have this basic understanding of human nature. An old saying in advertising goes: *Sell the sizzle, not the steak.*

The final section of your edited tape should be the music video, again this sets you apart from your competitors. It should be no longer in length than a three or so minute song that you feel is appropriate for the event. In the case of a wedding, some romantic song that you have interviewed the couple about and know they would like as their *music video*. Start with the wedding ceremony and end with the bride throwing the bouquet and of course, the final freeze frame of the two kissing, probably after they have shared their cake and have their faces covered with it. Fade out.

As you get more experience at doing this you will develop your own style and procedures. This is meant only as a starting place for ideas. Be inventive and try different things. One of the hardest things to do is to get a performance out of a non-actor, namely the guests that you interview. With practice you will discover how to coax light hearted humor out of them for the reel.

In the case of a bar mitzvah, keep in mind that this is the celebration of a boy becoming a man so think of ways of making him feel special, using the techniques mention above with the obvious alterations.

Promotional Videos

Promotional videos for a client's business are like producing a short movie without dramatic acting. This makes it a challenge to produce something that is interesting to watch. Merchants often think in 'yardage', the more they get, the cheaper it is for them. Unfortunately, that is not the case for the, sometimes reluctant, viewer of this video. So it is important to interview the client about the goals of the video before you start conceiving the theme of the video and the length.

A video that is nothing more than a long format commercial has a limited appeal to the potential viewer. Videos about the history and wonderfulness of the company, have a drop off interest rapidly after about eight minutes, with absolute snoring from the viewer occurring sometime after eleven minutes. The exception would be a video that explains how to build or put something together, or some complicated procedure.

Interviewing You Client

The importance of interviewing the client before hand can not be overstated. This is where you find out what the client is imagining the video to be and what you think it should be, based on your experience. Remember merchants think in yardage. "How much *quantity* can I get for my money?" The concept you want to sell to them is: How much *quality* can you give for the money? The following is a list of the kinds of questions you will want to ask your client about the video you hope to make for them:

☐ What is the purpose of the project?

☐ What is your idea of how long it should be?

☐ What is the place where the viewer will view the final product? [In their home, at the store, or a trade show?]

☐ Who is your potential customer?

☐ What are the important things you want the customer to know about your product or service?

☐ Where can we shoot this video for you?

☐ Can you supply employees to help us in this presentation? [Will they appear on camera?]

☐ Will the video require a hired talent as a spokesperson for the company or is there someone in the company who will supply this need? ["Hello, I am the president of..."]

☐ What is you idea for a timeline for producing this video? [Is there a deadline for a trade show for example?]

☐ Is this an informational tape or a sales tool?

☐ If it is an informational tape, how will it be used?

☐ If it is a sales tool, will it be for point of sale use or a call to action tool?

☐ Is this a tape that will be used only once or does it need to be structured so that it can be updated from time to time with new information?

☐ What is the budget you have with which to work?

These are the kinds of questions that someone with a lot of experience would ask a potential client. The client can immediately see that they are dealing with an experienced video producer by the nature of the questions asked and they can see that the producer knows how to go to the heart of what is important to the client.

Controlling The Client

By you asking these important questions right up front, you are saying that you know what you are doing, and that you have a lot of experience doing these kinds of projects. This puts the client at ease to know that they are dealing with a professional. You may blow this later if you ask for too little money for doing the project. *L'Oreal* said it best: "It cost a little more, but I am worth it.!" Asking for too little money says to the potential client that you do not really think you are worth more. On the other hand do not be arrogant about it, be professional. As long as we are talking about money, there is the consideration of a payment schedule. Your aim should be to have the client's capitol to work on not your own. That means getting a check up front to start production.

Payment Schedules

Any payment schedule that you are comfortable with will work, but you should strive for always working on their money, not yours. After you have worked out a budget, present it to the client in the form of an invoice. This is a plan that has worked well for others and does not make the client feel that they are taking too much risk:

☐ To start pre-production and script writing-10%

☐ Upon completion of a script and approval-10%

☐ Before start of production-50%

☐ Upon final approval of editing-20%

☐ Upon delivery of completed project-10%

The completion of the script and start of production may all start at once in which case you may want to alter the arrangement, slightly.

This kind of payment schedule puts the client at some small risk, not you. (Their only risk is if you take off with their money) The danger with having it the other way around is, you may not be able to pay your talent and crew at the time of their work, which is unprofessional and far more unpleasant than asking the client for money up front. It also avoids the opportunity for the client to renege after the project is compete, with you owing your cast and crew money. You can explain to the client that you have most of your expenses at the beginning of production and you will not see any money for yourself until the project is completed. This implies that you will only make about ten percent of the budget for yourself. That may be true, depending on how efficiently you work and how much money you waste along the way.

Developing The Script

Once you land the contract you must convert all of that talk into action in the form of a script. Hopefully, you took notes on all of those questions you asked at the meeting and have an idea about where to start developing the script. Referring back to the chapter on script writing you will remember the elements of creating a script.

☐   What is the purpose of the production?

☐   What are the basic elements of the production?

☐   We establish the kind of story we are about to tell.

☐   We establish the characters (In this case the company) we want our audience to know.

☐   We present the audience with our premise.

☐   We create a reason for our audience to keep watching or become more interested.

☐   Does the production lead to a call to action?

As you begin to create an outline for this script remember these questions to help guide you through that course of creating an outline:

1) What is my story in this promotional video?

2) How do I show it?

3) How do I 'sell' it to the audience?

4) How do I make it compelling and unique?

5) What is the climax of the important action?

6) How do I bring it to resolve?

7) Am I telling a story that the audience will remember or are these just connected shots with no theme?

Often, what sets you apart from the competition is your ability to put the video into a format that is pleasant to watch for the final end user. This comes from the time tested use of the dramatic storytelling format. How successful do you think a show like *America's Most Wanted*, starring John Walsh or *Unsolved Mysteries*, starring Robert Stack would have been, had they not used the re-enactment story technique? If they had either of those very charismatic personalities on camera, spouting dry facts, the show never would have made it through the pilot, much less several successful years on the networks and on-going syndication. Take a lesson from them and look for ways to tell your client's story in a way other than dry voice over facts while looking at factory footage. Not only will you create a better product, you will have a lot more fun doing it. It need not be scripted dialogue, 'silent movies' can still get the point over to your audience. Your job is to be creative in producing your video, otherwise a television news crew or a kid with a camcorder could do as well.

Notes:

Chapter Twenty-Seven

Producing Commercials

Producing commercials may not be for everyone. It is a difficult, competitive business, full of unforeseen problems that can wipe out any hope of profit on any given project. You can encounter clients that make it impossible for you to give them what they need, rather than what they think they want. If that does not scare you away, then you should also know that it can be some of the most exciting, rewarding work that you may be able to do.

Not unlike the promotional video for the client's business, your job is to sell their product or service. The commercial as stated in a previous chapter, involves telling a story beginning with a premise, and ending with a call to action. And like the promotional video in the previous chapter you must learn and understand what your client is selling so that you may help them develop a way to market that product or service. Making commercials adds the responsibility of making sure that what you create is worthy of the thousands of dollars the client must spend on top of your fees to promote their product on television. Two of the best ways of doing that are animals and humor, and with a little luck, both. So it helps to have a good sense of humor and have a feeling for what is funny and what is not. If you succeed, the client will be happy and viewers will gladly watch the commercial over and over again.

Marketing Your Client's Product

As you move into the realm of commercial production you are moving into the marketing arena. Commercials are not about advertising a product, they are about *marketing* a product. This is beyond the scope of this text on production, but it is such an essential concept to understand before engaging in the production of commercials, it is imperative to cover at least some aspects of this special kind of video production. Let us begin with understanding the difference between advertising and marketing.

A Brief Overview
Commerce is derived from existing business ˎand new business. New business comes from word of mouth, availability, or advertising. Since advertising is an out of pocket expense it should be critically considered from all aspects and unified for each of the media areas. If a mascot is used, then all advertising should have that common tie-in (RCA dog). If a logo is used to identify the product then it should always be present (Nike). In planning a campaign for a company, the identifying trademark should be established, if it does not already exist, and exploited in all advertising. This ingredient should be endearing and not overlooked as a hook or gimmick to gain audience recognition and acceptance.

Blanket advertising is largely a waste of money unless you are a Wal-Mart or Sears. Advertising agencies long ago discovered that the one ad in the paper does not get the expected response. Nor does that one TV commercial or that one page ad in the yellow pages, it is the combined impact of all of those elements. In fact, in most cases, a person looking in the yellow pages for who to call sees the mascot or logo and something in the back of their mind says 'Oh, that is who I want to call, I've heard of them...' They very seldom make a conscience connection that what they *really* know about the company is only what they have seen on TV, or newspaper and not a recommendation from a friend. If advertising is not a combined effort in most of these areas it should not be done at all except in yellow page advertising. That may be hard to take since you are in the video production business. However you have a responsibility to you client to help them get the most for their advertising dollar. You must take on the role of the advertising agency in cases where there is no agency to spearhead a media campaign, which you, as the video commercial producer is one part of that concerted effort.

Who is Your Client's Customer?

The first decision is to decide who is your client's customer? It should be a definition that can be stated in one simple sentence. For example let us use an excavation and rock supply company for our illustration. So their customers might be: "Contractors looking for big equipment." Or "Homeowners who need help landscaping their yard." Make a simple list of all the services your client's company now provides and any future services that could be added. Next, list what group could use those services if they knew about them. Once that clarification has been made, the next step is to begin targeting that specific group for the new business that will be generated from the advertising.

Highly successful businesses have one thing in common. They expanded their market by adding new product(s). There is a reason why this is true. Without this, once their market has been fully realized their <u>only</u> growth potential is through the growth of the businesses they serve. An easy example of this phenomenon is the McDonald's food chain. First, we saw the rise of this fast food enterprise for selling quick, cheap meals. As they saturated that market they targeted another segment of their potential market. Enter the 'Egg Mc Muffin'. They then were reaching a market to serve from the same investment with a whole new set of customers, the breakfast crowd. This, of course, was followed by Chicken Mc Nuggets (pseudo 'dinner' crowd), and so on and so on. So if you advise your client to expand their business by offering more services or services to a group of society that they are not presently serving, you are doing more than just making a commercial, based on what they thought they wanted. You are suggesting a whole new set of customers that you can help them reach through the marketing campaign you can create for your client. This is why you are getting into marketing when you think about making a commercial for your client. This concept is beyond even college level video production and should not be attempted without some other courses or experiences in advertising and marketing of products.

As you can see you have the potential of offering your clients much more than the average video producer and therefore something you should consider adding to your arsenal of weapons to aid your clients that other video producers do not have, namely more education in marketing.

Targeting Your Market

In this fast paced world we live, smart companies have discovered the key to great success, which is the knowledge that ultimately they are *problem solvers*. "I can't fix this leaking pipe in the wall, who do I call a plumber or a carpenter?" Who gets the call, the plumber, the carpenter or the Mr. Fix-it who can repair both the wall and the pipe and the homeowner stops worrying about the whole problem?

Taking this approach will open up your business potential because you are no longer doing business the way your competitors are doing business. You are solving problems for your clients, which is what more and more companies are wanting these days. So as you can see this applies to both you and your client.

In targeting your market, you also should consider creating a need and then filling it. Madison Avenue has been doing that for decades for the simple reason that there is a much bigger market in making people think they really need this widget, than just providing widgets. In many ways, the one ingredient that separates the profitable business from the 'break-even' one is having a clear understanding of the target market rather than a commonplace assumption that your products will sell themselves if only people knew about them. In other words, marketing campaigns create their own demand. This concept also is one that applies both to your potential clients and you as well.

Why You Will Be in Demand

It is important at this point to give you a little history of video production over the last few years. In the early nineties large corporations saw the potential of having their own in-house production facilities. For a quarter of a million dollar investment they could have cameras and editing bays that rivaled most television stations in quality. By hiring college students or others with some video experience and paying them far less than industry professionals, they could more than balance their expenditure in state-of-the-art equipment with the savings in labor. And they could enjoy the same quality of production and even increase their production output because they had an in-house production company. So much for corporate thinking, which sees the bottom line and never how they got to the bottom line.

Now, moving into the twenty-first century, most of those in-house production companies have faded away for several reasons. One, they were paying for staff and equipment overhead all the time and not using the production capability all of the time. Two, companies have discovered that health and welfare expenses are forcing them to down size many employees they can do without. And third, they did not get the industry professionals they were used to working with, they got people with little or no experience, and even less incentive. This creates a wonderful void for you to fill, now they are again looking for outside independent contractors to supply their video needs. They are looking for industry professionals, having learned that their in-house staff did not give them the same quality of creativity even though they had the high quality equipment.

Marketing, Not advertising

To fill this void you need to bring more to the table than just an excitement to want to do a good job for them, you need to bring them what they need rather than what they think they want, based on your concept of *marketing* their product rather than *advertising* their product.

An overall advertising campaign is more than a specific budget set aside for the available media outlets. It should be an in-depth study of the product line and how it impacts and targets a specific group or groups. This study should include the ancillary markets and spin-off products and be defined in its scope to meet the needs of the customers present and future. An example would be, using our excavation company example: Let's say your client's company has done several projects where the look of a house has been transformed in the target market and because of their know-how and artistic approach *and* your advertising, they find that their contractors(old business) begin to call and say that instead of just grading the front yard they want the total package, rocks, water elements, landscaping and bark chips. By suggesting to your client that they provide a turn key operation, they have eliminated part of the general contractor's job he does not want to be concerned with anyway (Becoming new business). The only products they are not currently providing are plants that could be subcontracted out with a supervising percentage added to cover their trouble. Your client realizes they can provide much more-namely, *problem solving.*

The advertising campaign is much more involved than just running ads, it is a part of the overall business plan that is aimed at a specific market. A market that has been researched by you and defined by the extent of the products offered.

Media Resources

Local advertising opportunities include newspapers, television, radio, yellow pages, billboard and on-site displays. They all have their place and solve particular needs. They are your competitors for your client's advertising dollar. You may want to express the follow to your potential client in your own words as a selling point for your services:

☐ Newspaper advertising is an effective way of announcing something special and keeping their name in the public's mind. It is greatly limited because fewer and fewer people have the time to read the paper and the ones that do could easily miss your ad.

☐ Television advertising has one of the greatest impacts on the public for a number of reasons. First, it reaches a much larger audience. Second, it targets a specific audience through proper selection of cable channels and times. Third, it places a notion of celebrity in the mind of the audience that seems to be unique to our culture. "These people must be important they advertise on TV and that's expensive!" Actually, it is probably the cheapest cost per new customer bargain they can get because you can target their potential market so well.

☐ Radio advertising has the opportunity to reach a captive audience, the ones trapped in their vehicles and on job sites. Because it is blanket advertising and rivals TV advertising in cost it should be examined carefully to judge its true potential. In other words forget it, it is direct competition with your services and has only blanket impact on a nonspecific audience.

☐ Yellow page advertising is expensive and a must for all the obvious reasons. As stated previously, it should be part of the overall campaign designed toward customer recognition at the time of the first contact with their business.

☐ Billboard advertising is also blanket advertising and should be used like newspaper advertising to announce specific specials or keep their company's name in the mind of the public. What is worthy of billboard advertising is its visual impact. The right picture of their product or service can be just the thing to move someone to call. An on-site billboard is an expensive investment but has remarkable possibilities. They own it, it is seen by every driver by the site, it is a reminder to those who have been impacted by your TV advertising at the perfect time to pull in, and it showcases the other products they have on display at the site.

☐ On-site displays are an expensive investment but also create a desire in the mind of the driver passing by. A good example of this phenomenon is the popularity of the kitchen remodel magazines. Most people don't really know what exactly they want but they know when they see it that that is exactly what they were imagining. With the right displays with enough detail, people will stop and that can be the beginning.

Some Final Thoughts On Marketing to Your Clients

As a company grows it reaches a critical mass at which point it remains the same for years or declines or in some rare cases it explodes into something far greater than anyone could have imagined. You may be in a position to help them do just that. An example is the story of an overworked waitress at a small cafe. The owner insisted that she make pies at home because he had no one else or any other source for them. Soon, she made pies for others and eventually quit her job waiting tables and started a pie company for restaurants. And using the formula mentioned above expanded to provide new 'products' and new ways of marketing them. Several years ago the ex-waitress sold her company to some giant corporation for Ninety Million Dollars. Oh, the waitresses' name? Maybe you have heard of her, *Marie Callendar*.

The formula works.

Using these illustrations or ones like them can go a long way toward convincing your client to do more than shoot a commercial. It can be a springboard toward a marketing campaign that you will be in charge of for your clients. It is the beginning for you to have a greater impact on the community in which you live and work. Before long you will find more and more clients will be coming to you because you do more than shoot commercials, you solve problems for them. And that is exactly what people want these days. Companies that are *problem solvers*.

Chapter Twenty-Eight

Producing Documentaries

For decades the real training ground for young filmmakers was the documentary. There was at one time a number of organizations that funded films for various causes. To some degree that has become more difficult to obtain. At the same time with the acceptance of video for 'filming' these documentaries it has become possible to produce such projects for far less expense. The documentary has many of the qualities of a commercial and a dramatic story, along with a promotional film thrown in. Unlike the other type projects, the documentary requires a strong dependence on the ability and experience of the editor to make the project work.

The Nature of Documentaries

The very nature of the documentary encourages one to shoot first and ask questions later, so to speak. As a veteran of countless documentaries, having used that technique, I can say that it is a difficult job to manage all of the visual information that is generated from that shooting style. Shooting ratios from twenty to over a hundred to one are easy to have before the project is completely shot and ready to edit. The source of this problem for the most part comes from working with non-actors. The process usually involves takes and re-takes because they are not sure what to say on camera. The other footage waster comes from the interviewer asking a question after the camera has started and then waiting for the interviewee to collect their thoughts to answer. There are ways to minimize this problem that will be discussed within this chapter.

It would be noble if documentaries always took the approach of not having a predisposed point of view before beginning. That seldom is the case, the very nature of the documentary is to prove some point of view. If you interview any number of people about any given subject you will get more than one point of view. If the 'poll' has only two points of view and the total number of people polled indicates that about half believe one thing and half believe the other, which is the truth? That is where the filmmaker "fiddles" with the outcome in any number of ways. For example, the editor or filmmaker might use only the interviews of one group that were not well educated to present one point of view in a clumsy way, and use well educated ones who speak in an articulate way to bolster up the other point of view that they want the audience to believe is the right one. Another way is to use several of one point of view and only a few of the others. The way that a question is posed can also affect the way that one side will look in presenting what they believe. Few politicians, police officers, lawyers, or doctors can hold up to the scrutiny of clever editing. I have tremendous respect and admiration for the late Don Hewitt, the renowned producer of *60 Minutes*. Over the several decades of the show he has exposed many who needed their dirty deeds uncovered. It would be naive to not understand that they too can fiddle with the outcome whenever they want. It is the very nature of "He said, she said" kind of situations.

One of the best documentaries ever produced, called *Scared Straight*, was a documentary about teens who had been arrested who were taken to a maximum penitentiary and subjected to killers who told them what would happen to them if they ended up in prison with them. Some very tough kids ended up crying they were so scared. Many of the teens that went through the program were never arrested again. Hopefully, some teens that saw the documentary got the message without having to experience it first hand. It is an excellent teaching tool for those who are interested in making documentaries.

Organizational Thinking

To begin a documentary, you first want to have a premise that you believe to be true. It could be: *There is a rise in the crime rate in the inner city.* Or perhaps: *Local manufacturer caught polluting our river water.* Or you might have seen a newspaper article that triggered an idea such as: *Teen pregnancy is on the decline thanks to better education.*

The second step is to research the topic to get more facts from whatever sources you have at your disposal, newspaper articles, magazines, Internet, books, television news programs and interviews with people involved.

Once all of these thoughts and notes have been collected, you want to begin writing your 'story' by starting with your premise. As you can see, the techniques that we presented in the first chapter about learning how to tell a story just keeps coming back to you in the same form, that is, why it is so important to learn about premise, or else factors and resolve, they are the basis for all cinematic presentations.

The third step is to take all of your research material and decide on your point of view. For an example, we will use: *Local manufacturer caught polluting our river water.* What are some of your point of view choices?

☐ The plant is willfully polluting the water.

☐ The plant has not put proper safeguards in place to know if they are polluting.

☐ The local governmental agency is not policing the environment as mandated, and therefore inviting violations because of negligent inspections.

☐ The plant foreman has allowed the pollution in order to meet quotas and get operational cost savings kickbacks for himself.

Within any one of those possibilities there are any number of sub possibilities such as the plant was there first and feels they have a right to keep on polluting. Or a local inspector has been looking the other way and taking kickbacks under the table. Or even the company is actually secretly partly owned by the mayor who has made sure nothing would stop their profit flow and has covered up the problem for years.

What is the truth? At this point you do not know. By the time your program airs, you may still not know the truth. As you develop your premise, you will begin to see certain things come to life in your investigation. Some of us who have done these kinds of things call this a 'tell'. A term made popular from the movie *House of Games* by David Mamet. The story of a small band of con artists. A tell is when a person says one thing and their body language or eye movement says the opposite. As you develop your awareness in interviewing people about a touchy subject, you will begin to see these 'tells' come out. Sometimes you do not need a tell to know you are on to something, like when they invite you to leave as soon as you ask them if there *is* a pollution problem at the plant.

This kind of gorilla filmmaking is not for the faint of heart, and it can be dangerous to your health, if you start asking the wrong people the wrong questions. There is a reason this subject has been used in more than one action/adventure movie.

Anyone appearing on camera must sign an artist release. This is a legal document that gives the filmmaker the right to use their likeness for whatever purpose the filmmaker chooses. [See appendix] You have probably heard at one time or another about a celebrity who posed nude and years later it came back to haunt them. This is the reason that happens, the photographer got the release at the time of the photo shoot and therefore there is nothing the celebrity can do about it, even years later. How this applies to you is that you must do the same thing. Now if you ask for the release to be signed after you shoot an interview, the subject can decline if they feel that you are not going to put them in the best light. If you get the release signed before you start the interview when everyone is all friendly and cordial, then there is nothing they can do about it except strong arm it back from you after you make them look bad. Your call. [My advice: Get it on camera, whatever happens.]

The same goes for your tactics in general in trying to get your shots. If you call the plant and say that you are doing a documentary on their pollution, there is a real good chance they will not let you shoot. If you come by with your cameras and ask what they make there and could you shoot scenes of their business, they might let you film if they have nothing to hide. By gushing such questions as: "Do you hire a lot of local people?", or: "Does the local economy depend on this plant?", or even: "This plant represents several generations of livelihood for families here, right?" You may endear yourself long enough to get what you want in coverage and provide a background for asking for an interview later. When it comes time for the interview at a later time, you will want to be up front about where you are heading. They have a right to know and be asked up front how they respond to the claims against them. They may choose to not be interviewed at all, or only limited, pre-decided questions or may have their attorney speak for them. At least you will have cutaway footage from your first on-site shoot. It is never wise to trespass on private property or do anything illegal to get your shots and interviews. There are enough legal ways to make cutting edge documentaries without resorting to unlawful methods. After all, criminal acts may be the subject of what you are trying to expose about them.

Required viewing for anyone making a documentary is to watch several episodes of *60 Minutes*. Careful scrutiny of that program will teach you more than ten chapters in this book on the subject. They do three stories of about fifteen minutes in length each. There is a reason for this. People tire of anything longer than that. Keep that in mind as you plan your story and its length. If you budget the time allotment before you start and stick to it, you will find that instead of rambling and losing focus on what is important, you will be cutting it down to the core to stay within that time budget. You will learn to be your own Don Hewitt. Rambling also causes your audience to lose focus and get caught up in unimportant side issues. If you do that enough, you will lose them altogether. Investigative reporters on the air keep the focus on the point they want made, when they interview some guest 'victim'.

Short Cut to the Finished Product
There is a technique which greatly speeds up the process of making a documentary, and that is to transcribe all of the spoken words from interviews and voice over information to paper, ideally, the word processor.

You will have a 'book' that is a story of what you want the audience to know. Now edit the book. Tell your story as though it is a written story. It does not matter if one paragraph is a voice over and the next is an on camera interview. It does not matter if you cut up the interview so that you have concise sentences that are not continuous, if they tell the story in the shortest, clearest way possible even though in pictures it is all jumbled up. You will be able to put it together later with cutaways and graphics and dissolves. When it reads clearly and in a few words, you have a good story. Now you can edit from the printed page and conform your footage to match the printed copy. There will be places that you wonder how you can possibly fill the void with a picture, but it will come to you and it will work. And you will finish the project much sooner than if you played in the edit room with pieces that make no sense without a written story to follow.

Once the 'story' is complete on paper comes the difficult job of creating a flowing documentary in visuals and sound from that road map. There is only one way to do that.

The Rough Cut

First, record the voice over artist's copy from your scripted voice over sections. This recording should be paced at a speed that seems natural and yet moves along quickly to keep the interest up for the audience.

Second, lay down the on camera interviews, following your script. At this point, disregard the fact that the picture jumps from one shot to the next. What you want right now is to have the voice of the interviewee flow as normal as possible. This is assuming that from time to time there will be cases where what the subject said last, may come up first in the new written version of their interview. As you play this section of the documentary you will think it looks like one big mess. Just trust me for now, it will all come together as we go through each step.

Make it Work as a Radio Program First

Third, review the documentary from start to finish and see how it compares to the script. What I have done on many occasions is to play the video and look at the script to see that I have not left out whole sections. It also keeps me from panicking by watching the screen and seeing juxtaposition shots abounding. Once you are sure that nothing has been left out, you want to watch it for pacing. Is the voice over too slow? Too rushed? Have you told your story as a radio program? If the answer is yes and you are happy with the audio side of the program it is time to watch it for picture replacement ideas.

Now as you watch your rough cut of the show you will see sections where it sounds right but the screen will have a subject being interviewed with pictures jump cutting from shot to shot. To make it easy to visualize this problem, let us say that in the given section we are describing we have five cuts of the subject. These five cuts were taken from a long interview that lasted two minutes, in this edited down version the whole section lasts thirty seconds. As subjects talk, they will move their heads, scratch their face, and fix their hair. As we have cut this piece, all of those things happened and there is no hope of matching these sections from cut to cut. It does not matter. Let us also say that cuts one, two and four have been moved around so that the order now is five, one, four, three and we end the interview on what was said second. Since you knew this sort of thing would happen, when you were shooting the subject, you were sure to shoot additional footage of cutaways. Maybe a close up of their hands, the back of their head as they spoke, maybe a cutaway which refers to the subject being discussed with the subject in the same shot. So you have someplace to go. Along with this extra footage you also have generic footage of say the factory interior footage you shot, remember? Now you see why I had you shoot that footage.

Learning how to Insert

So we start with (new) cut number one, it lasts for six seconds. Just long enough to dissolve in their name as a graphic and back out again. At six seconds, we cut to the wide shot of the factory, with the river in the foreground. This shot covers the second shot of the subject talking so we do not see the face jump on the screen The second piece lasts for five seconds, which is just about the right amount of time for the cutaway to the factory. As the second piece ends the picture would jump again as we start section three. Instead, we hold the factory shot until three starts and then cut back to the on camera shot of the interviewee still talking. As this section three ends there will be another jump so we splice in a new shot, maybe a rear shot of the person talking as cut number four begins. We hold on this cutaway for two seconds and then return to take four. It flows nicely and the audience still has not detected any picture jumps. At the end of section four we have another jump coming up as it goes into section five. One second before the picture jump we cut away to the factory interior showing a point being made by the interviewee, holding on this cutaway as we move into the last section. Maybe we hold this cutaway for a total of three seconds so that two seconds into the fifth section we cut back to the person talking. We stay on this cut until the end of the interview for this section of the documentary . So we have gone from an interview with a person whose sound made perfect sense, but the picture jumped from one cut to the next. Now we have an interview whose picture flows smoothly. It started with a picture of the person talking, we added a nice graphic announcing who they were, six seconds in, we cut to a shot of the factory, then back to the person talking. While they were talking we cut to a brief shot of the back of their head where the audience may or may not have noticed a mismatch in the person's gestures, back to their face for a few more seconds, then a cut of the inside of the factory which made perfect sense because that is what they were talking about, and finally back to the person on camera for the last few seconds of the interview. It is that simple. Five sections that did not match, repaired with three brief cutaways to fix them, and in fact, made it more interesting than watching a talking head for thirty boring seconds. And certainly more interesting than two minute interview that we might have had because we were afraid to cut into smaller sections because of jump cutting. Lazy editors use the wipe method where they sneak out of one cut to the next with that cheesy wipe so you don't see the jump. Which is worse?

The explanation described above will make your program look professional, and ultimately be much more satisfying for you and your audience.

Let me explain briefly the other way of doing this. It has been done by others for decades. If you like to work harder and spend more money editing, this is for you: First you rough cut the section you are working on by putting visuals together at some pace or rhythm that seems right to you. Then you hire a voice over artist and book a session at a recording studio that can play your footage to the artist as he reads the copy. He paces his voice over to match your rough-cut footage needing several takes to get it right, using a lot of studio time. Back at your edit facility, you put the two together and then begin inner cutting this pre-edited section with interviews which you cut into these voice over sections. Once that is done if the rhythm seems off or the writing needs adjusting, you hire the voice over artist and book another session to re-record his voice over at the new pace or with the new copy or both. You then re-edit the voice over and see if it is better paced for the program. Voice over artists much prefer the latter way of doing it because they get paid twice for the same work. So does the recording studio. The first way requires you to write the voice over and imagine the kinds of pictures you want to place with these voice overs. And you have to determine in advance what is important to the story you want to tell. That is why I refer to it as a radio program. The best way to leave you some breathing room is to structure the voice over copy into clear separate sections or paragraphs. You can adjust the pause of the artist in the editing suite to lengthen a shot that you want to hold longer. Or you can tuck up the pauses if you want to shorten sections of the voice overs. The voice over artist does not have to watch a monitor of your work to match your pace. He or she is a professional and you can match their natural pace much better. This is why it is so important to work from a script. Like every other kind of project, the story is what is essential to get across to your audience. Hard to believe it, but there are people in the documentary business that will swear to you the latter way is the only way. Not knowing any better the first time out, I did it that way.

It took forever. After that, thanks to the brilliance of Dr. Keith Phillips, the President of World Impact, who had written several books, we created our documentaries as a book first, then a 'radio show' and finally as finished films and years later as video presentations. It saved thousands of dollars and months of work. Unnecessary work.

Final Thoughts

There seems to be a strong tendency among beginners to cut picture first and sound second. To me, it just will not work that way because you can not edit a person's sentences by cutting in between words and change their pacing or how long it takes them to say something. So if it is wrong, you have to re-record it. You can easily cut the picture to match the time that it takes them to say it. Why work so hard just so you can do it backwards? Editing is hard enough without *extra* work.

Chapter Twenty-Nine

Being Professional

In part three of this text we have covered several topics on filmmaking that are aimed at what you will most likely encounter in the real world of production. As you enter that work force you may be an employee of a large production facility or even a small one working with local merchants. You may find yourself thrown into the 'lion's den' of working on your own with your individual clients. In any case, the experience gained from this text in a class room learning situation will give you an understanding which will better prepare you for the actual workplace. You may find that because you do have an understanding of the intricacies of each of the types of projects covered in the last few chapters, that you will rise much faster in that company. Companies are always on the lookout for young talent that act professionally and can take responsibility to produce high-quality results for the employer. In this chapter we will discuss a number of issues that would not fit as part of any other chapter, but are very essential in the production world.

Starting On Time

Whether you are working part time at a fast food restaurant, or printing shop, you more than likely have a habit of getting to work within a few minutes on either side of your scheduled start time. You have a routine and you know how long it takes you to get there each day so you time it as closely as possible. If you do not have your own transportation and must rely on public transportation, you probably even have that timed so that you do not spend any more time than necessary waiting at work. If you are working on a feature film on location or some other production that does not require a standard start time, it is important that you get into the habit of being at work at least fifteen minutes early. Feature films generally do not always have the same start time for a number of reasons. Some days they might start at six-thirty in the morning and at other times four in the afternoon and go all night. If the shooting schedule requires it, the company may spend only a day or less at the same location. That means that each day you may be traveling to a different part of the city, parking a long way from the actual location of the shooting area, and encountering tourists blocking your way as they try to get a closer look at a movie being made. If the company is also causing traffic slow downs for the normal residents in the area, that could also slow things down even more. All of these factors make it imperative that you get to work with plenty of time to spare in case any one of these possibilities slow you from being where you are suppose to be at the call time. Professionals get to work fifteen to thirty minutes early every day of production. It is a great time to network, relax and have coffee, find out what is going on that day and park in a better spot than you would have if you were on time or a little late. Very often the parking area fills up before everyone arrives so alternate parking must be found at the last minute. Just when you are already late you have the hassle of driving to another spot to park that is farther away and makes you even more late than you were. This kind of stress makes the whole day less pleasant, and labels you as undependable.

Sitting Down on the Job

We have all seen director's chairs on locations with the actor's name on the back. There is a reason why that actor, director, producer, prop man, D.P. or make up artist's name is on that chair. For whatever reason, the company feels they need a chair close to the action. You will also quickly notice that it does not have your name on it. That should be a clue that you should not sit in a chair with someone else's name on it. There may also be other chairs without names on them, this is because the company has rented these chairs for the department heads and it is too expensive to send the chairs out for name printing. Unless you are a department head such as the ones listed above or the art department head, the gaffer, stunt coordinator, hair or wardrobe. There is a good chance they were not considering you when they ordered chairs. Having a chair on the set is something that is earned from years of being in the business. Respect that tradition of providing chairs only for department heads and look forward to the day that they will provide one for you. Until then, stay out of other people's chairs unless you want to be embarrassed by being asked to get up by a cranky prop man who was not crazy about setting up all of those chairs to start with. This is true even if all of the chairs are empty.

About Pigging Out

Another time honored tradition is the order in which people are served a meal on location. When lunch or dinner is called everyone files to the catering truck or catering tables set up with food, it is tradition to let the department heads move slightly ahead of you as they approach the line. This is a more subtle protocol to learn.

Basically, you just do not want to break and run for the line. You will see some do it, but of course you will not. Slipping into line just behind your department head is probably a good idea. On some shoots, the 1st A.D. will announce who he or she wants to eat first, either the actors so they can finish first and get to make up, or the gaffer's team so they can get back early and set lights. Seconds or extra helpings should occur only after everyone has been fed because the cater always runs a little short if crew members help themselves to too much food. Be polite and not a jerk when in doubt. The same goes for the coffee and pastry table in the morning. It is there as a courtesy for everyone to enjoy, it is not there to subsidize your breakfast budget.

A Little Less Noise, Please

Hopefully you will experience sound recording before the day that you work on a professional sound stage or location. On the sound stage it is vital that you are aware of how sensitive the mics can be. You want to respect the whirling red light when you see one. It means just what you think it does. Do not enter. You may have to wait several minutes before you can open the sound stage door. If you think: "Gee they won't hear me enter, I'll be very quiet opening the door." POP!

The doors make a loud pop when entering because of the blowers that quietly remove the hot air from the lights. It is a sound you would never notice until making it during a take and hear someone yell: "Cut and who opened the door while the red light was on?"

It is a good idea to freeze when you hear the words: "And action." If your feet grind the sand under your feet during a take you will often see the 1st. A.D. frowning at you as you look up from your feet, in amazement that you could have possibly made any sound at all. It should go without saying that you never talk or even whisper during a take. For most, these things seem obvious and a waste of time to mention them. This is written for the few that never seem to think about others. You know the ones of which I speak.

While on the subject of do's and don'ts': There are more than a few actors, some who are celebrities and several who are not, that take exception to some crew member standing in their line of sight, picking their nose or worse, as the actor works in a scene. It can be understandably distracting to them. MOVE!

Never sit on furniture in the set that will be photographed. The art department does not like it and the furniture was not brought there for your enjoyment. Sit on an apple box if one is available. An apple box is a plywood box measuring eight inches by twelve inches by eighteen inches approximately, used for all sorts of things on a movie set. So named because they are about the size of boxes used to pack freshly picked apples.

Do Not Phone Home

Sound stages all have phones. They are for communication from the production office to the set. Sometimes they are needed for the assistant director's team to get in touch with players who are not on set, to call the cater about their arrival time, film stock house to get an emergency order to them and a thousand other reasons except one, enhancing your personal life through phone conversations. Actors are the worse abusers of the stage phone, calling their agent every five minutes to see if they have an interview. What everyone seems to forget is that the production office can not get through to the stage if it is always busy. Do not use the phone and discourage others from using the phone. Do not give out the number for your friends to call you there.

These are things that are nice to find out about before your big first day on the set. And you will be glad that you know about them in advance, as you watch others being embarrassed that were not forewarned.

Chapter Thirty

A New Direction

At the beginning of this course, you may have not known for sure where this text might go, or perhaps you expected a hands on experience in camera and technical operation only. There are such curriculum text available to you for that kind of instruction. Learning the craft is never a waste of time, but time is precious because you have so little of it in a classroom situation. It is vital that you learn certain skills in the most economical, and professional way. For that reason, the text herewith has been approached in a slightly different way, namely, as a way to learn a useful skill in an ever changing industry. Man has not always had camcorders, motion picture equipment, or even amphitheaters for plays. But man has always had a story to tell an audience, be that a large tribe or a small group gathered around a campfire. So telling a good story will always be in demand no matter what the medium may be or become in the near future. That storytelling is the basis for broadcasting and film production. The basics have been given to you in this text with the hope that you, on your own would seek out more information about any given subject or area mentioned in this text. The underlining theme throughout has been the importance of the script, and that everything in production starts with a script. Even a wedding or a bar mitzvah has a script when you convert what you shot to a video presentation. Why this was done was to give you the secret formula for success in production work. You now will be able to look at the core of any production problem and see the solution that the others may not see because they have not learned to look deeper into the story structure of the problem. If you truly understand what has been done here you will learn to ask yourself this question: "What are we trying to say here to our audience?" When you start to ask those kinds of questions the answers will come more quickly and more clearly.

There are some rules for success that you should remember as you start down this exciting road, they begin with:

☐ Take notes for future reference on the many subjects related to this craft.

☐ If there is anything mentioned in this book or any other book you own that will be of help to you later, highlight it with highlight marker so you may find it at a glance. Refer to these things often as a reminder.

☐ Begin collecting a good professional library of books on the subjects mentioned in this book. (Beginning with *Writing the Script* by Wells Root, Holt, Rinehart and Winston, New York)

☐ Always have your mind tuned to a good idea for a story when you hear it, whether it is the news, a newspaper, or a friend. Or even something you overhear on a bus or subway.

☐ Stay informed about this craft by attending workshops, trade shows, television programs and publications for this industry.

☐ When you have the free time, watch others doing this kind of work, like watching movies being made in your town on the streets.

☐ Never allow yourself to stop the learning process, it is a journey, not a destination.

☐ Give back what you have learned along the way to future generations by getting involved with student groups. They will teach <u>you</u> more than you can imagine.

Video and film production is not for everyone, you may have taken this course for credit only. You may have discovered a love for filmmaking that you never knew existed, or you may have just had an interesting time and discovered that it is not for you as a life's work. What you will have is a new understanding for some things that may help you in the career that you do choose. Writing company reports that might otherwise have been painfully boring, or video presentations for company business that adds humor or insight that might otherwise not have been there. In any case, this was not a waste of time. The skills given by the text and your instructor or teacher will be of use in ways that you yet understand.

What may not be written outwardly in the text of this book is my desire to see you succeed though I will never know you personally, to give you hope and inspiration to try something that parents and others may think is unrealistic as a goal or career. Only you can judge what potential is there for you. If you never try you will never know what could have been. Believe in yourself against all odds and you will succeed. Only those who keep giving it their all become the leaders we all admire, no matter what the career or discipline may be. The future is yours.

The future is Now.

I look forward to seeing a movie *you* have made <u>when</u> (not if) it comes to a theatre near me or is presented on TV.

If you have purchased this book not as a textbook for a class you are taking but as a study source for the desire you have to learn filmmaking, I would encourage you to find others of like minds and create your own study group. Follow the text that you have read and then put it to work by going over the chapters with your group and doing the exercises together just as though you are in a college or high school class. It will not be any different than a college course and you will learn just as much as you would if this were a course for credit. Filmmaking is a team effort so working with others that want to learn filmmaking is the best way for you to learn and grow.

Appendix

The 'Wrap'

Wrapping you production at the end of the day requires several tasks that should be organized and completed before leaving for the day.

- ❑ Preparing a Call Sheet for the next day's shooting.
- ❑ Make sure everyone gets their call sheet before leaving.
- ❑ All returns and pick ups for the next day's shooting should be arranged. In the case of shooting on film, delivery of the negative to the lab and ordering film stock pick up should also be considered.
- ❑ Alert catering what the needs will be for the next day.
- ❑ Clean up location/set and make an idiot check to see that nothing is left behind or needs to be put away-as needed.
- ❑ Check to see that communication devices are being accounted for and in chargers for the next day.
- ❑ Check dressing rooms for wardrobe and clean as needed, in the case of a practical location, make sure you sign off with the owner that all is back as before you arrived on their property.

As well as a typical Call Sheet there are other standard forms on the following pages that will be of use to you for your production. Feel free to change these simple guide line forms to suit your own unique needs.

CALL SHEET

Production Company_____ Date_____

Show_____ Director _____

Prod Mgr _____ Producer _____

Prod# _____ Day# _____Out of_____ Location _____

Crew Call_____ Leaving Call_____ Shoot Call_____

SET DESCRIPTION	SCENE #	CAST	D/N	PAGES	LOCATION

CAST	PART OF	LEAVE	MAKEUP	SET CALL	REMARKS

ATMOSPHERE & STAND-INS

_____

_____

_____

_____

Assistant Director _____Unit Manager_____

Copy and change as needed by your particular needs

EDL Production_____Page____of_____

Scene _____ Date_____

#	Media	IN	OUT	DUR	Video	Audio	Description	FX

Talent Release:

TALENT RELEASE

I understand the video or film being taken of me on this date_____I hereby
assign and authorize the producer, _____the right (All Rights) in and to
such video or film. I also authorize said producer, without limitation, the right to
reproduce, copy, exhibit-publish or distribute any such production, and waive all
rights or claims I may have against your organization and/or any of its Affiliates,
Subsidiaries, or Assignees other than as stated in this agreement.

_____   _____
  Signature of Talent   Signature of Producer(s)

_____
  Date

Change to suit your particular needs, also find other samples on-line

The author would like to thank Carolyn and Dan Hennings of World Impact, TUMI, Wichita Kansas, for their help in preparing this book for printing. I could not have done it without their tireless help.

William Mims

Made in the USA
Monee, IL
10 September 2021

77691882R00174